Poetry In Motion

Southern England
Edited by Donna Samworth

CW00762174

 Young**Writers**

First published in Great Britain in 2004 by:
Young Writers
Remus House
Coltsfoot Drive
Peterborough
PE2 9JX
Telephone: 01733 890066
Website: www.youngwriters.co.uk

SB ISBN 1 84460 399 7

Foreword

This year, the Young Writers' 'Poetry In Motion' competition proudly presents a showcase of the best poetic talent selected from over 40,000 up-and-coming writers nationwide.

Young Writers was established in 1991 to promote the reading and writing of poetry within schools and to the youth of today. Our books nurture and inspire confidence in the ability of young writers and provide a snapshot of poems written in schools and at home by budding poets of the future.

The thought effort, imagination and hard work put into each poem impressed us all and the task of selecting poems was a difficult but nevertheless enjoyable experience.

We hope you are as pleased as we are with the final selection and that you and your family continue to be entertained with *Poetry In Motion Southern England* for many years to come.

Contents

Dormers Wells High School, Southall

Amy McGinness (11)	19
Jennifer Ingole (13)	20
Tara McBeth (16)	20
Ibran Ahmed (13)	21
Nickeisha Roberts (12)	21
Ryan Willmer (13)	22
Shaniqua B Esprit (13)	22
Roma Givane (14)	23
Amarjit Syan (14)	23
Janani Arulrajah (12)	24
Zahra Abbas (12)	24
Amar Singh Ruprah (11)	25
Ibrahim Aden (11)	25
Roger Smith (11)	26
Ceren Apaydin	26
Edwin Akoto (11)	27
Jasmine Porter (12)	27
Imran Shah (13)	28
Rubeena Pitchey (14)	28
Latoya Samantha Wilson (13)	29
Rakesh Gogna (14)	29
Bile Abdulle (12)	30
Temitayo Phillips (15)	31
Aisha Harris (12)	31
Mandy-Lee Boyd (13)	32
Aissa Salimo (14)	32
Uzma Saleem (14)	33
Kancha Mbwengele (15)	34
Namneet Preenie Gill (15)	35
Charlene Badibanga (13)	36
Harmeet Gill (13)	37
Stacey Moles (13)	37
Charly Creagh (14)	38
Saad Khan (14)	39
Uljit Singh Sarna (15)	39
Basharat Hussain (13)	40
Chris Moles (13)	40
Dimple Gohil (15)	41
Rajwant Cheema (14)	41
Patrish Lionel (14)	42

Downside Middle School, Newport, Isle of Wight

Hartsdown Technology College, Margate

Jack Mackins (11)	62
Cara Mei Kember (12)	62
Lauren Callaghan (11)	63
Fairlie Ward (11)	63
Lucy Foster (11)	63
Bradley Thompson (13)	64
Christina Skillen (11)	64
Jasmine Ayles (11)	65
David Sims (11)	65
Ben Turner (13)	66
Darren Wynne (13)	66
Benjamin Mason (13)	67
Sophie Healy (13)	67
Sean Hampton (12)	68
Katie Chelton (12)	68
Sian Vizzard (11)	69
Alisha Thornett (13)	69
Charlene Welsh (11)	70
Daniel Dean (11)	70
Melissa Hamer (12)	71
Jamie Daniel (13)	71
Jason Williams (11)	72
Emily Wonford (12)	72
Rebekah Tumber (12)	73
Lauren Lipscomb (13)	73
Chris David Pannell (12)	74
Siobhan Pretty (11)	74
Laura Palmer (12)	75
Nicholas Carrington (13)	75
Leigh Page (12)	76
Deni Arklie (11)	77
Simon Watts (12)	78
Alex Moore (11)	78
Hannah Taylor (12)	79
Katie Brown (12)	80
Samantha May (12)	81
Jessica Gadsden (11)	81
Matthew Richardson (12)	82
Bethany Wigley (13)	82
Jade Jewell (11)	83
Rebecca Stevens (11)	83

Rebecca Lawrence (13)   83
Adam Chapman (12)   84
Talos Williams (13)   84
Hannah Young (12)   85
Mark Roberts (12)   86
Zoe Heavey (12)   87
Robert Mason (11)   87

Invicta Grammar School for Girls, Maidstone
Jasmine Jakubowski (11)   88
Samantha Woolley (11)   88
Clara Metcalfe (11)   89
Katie Wood (12)   90
Amy Kemp (11)   90
Jorjia Croucher (11)   91
Francesca North (11)   91
Alix Rowe (11)   92
Kelly Inman (11)   92
Charlotte Friend (11)   93
Emily Mayhew (11)   94
Saira Ahmed (11)   94
Alice Whittaker (11)   95
Holly Saunders (12)   95
Lauren Elphick (11)   96
Selina Towers (11)   97
Poppy Partridge (11)   97
Rebecca Abbott (11)   98
Georgina Owen (11)   98
Rhian Stone (11)   99
Hannah Turner (11)   99
Leah Roberts (11)   100
Rosie Gouldsworthy (11)   100
Charlotte Sheppard (11)   101
Rhiannon Prosser (11)   101
Claire Street (11)   102
Madeleine Starks (11)   102
Natasha Johnson (11)   103
Kerry Cheeseman (11)   103
Bethany Lucas (11)   104
Megan Libbeter (11)   104
Charlotte Adamson (11)   105

Lauren Billington (11)	106
Holly Louise Froud (11)	106
Georgina Haynes (12)	107
Michelle Thompson (11)	107
Georgina Evans (11)	108
Phebe Dwyer (11)	109

King Ethelbert School, Birchington
Jordana Parker (14)	110
Marc Sayer (11)	110
Thomas Jordan (11)	111
Grant Rutter	111
Luke Spinks (11)	112
John Dean (11)	112
Shauni White (11)	113
Paige White (11)	114
Lucy Amos (11)	114
Dean Parsons (11)	115
Sam Clarke (11)	116
Lewis Ward Peakall (11)	116
Kayleigh Chapman (13)	117
Adam Pacey (11)	117
Lannah Marshall (11)	118
Clair Booker (15)	119
Sarah Mitchell (13)	120
Thomas Gibson (11)	120
Gemma Lee (13)	121
Tyrrell Martin (12)	121
Sian Fields (14)	122
Sarah Barar (14)	122
Natasha Jordan (11)	123
Shauni White (11)	123
Paige White (11)	123
Christopher Nicholls (14)	124
Naomi Davis (12)	124
Kayleigh Morris (14)	125
Jay Dawson (14)	125
Amy Johncock (14)	126
Thomas Howe (11)	126
Christian Blow (14)	127
Hayley Morgan (13)	127

St Mary's Middle School, Dorchester
Hannah Downton (12)   145

Solent Middle School, Cowes
Oliver Denton (11)   145
James Tomkins (12)   146
Melanie Rock (11)   146
Sam Tyson (11)   147
Zoe Minshull (11)   147
Adam Mitchell (12)   148
Josh Pointing (12)   149
Helen Baggett (12)   150
Ben Green (12)   151
Rachel Bennett (12)   152
Joe Moody (11)   153

Sunbury Manor School, Subury-on-Thames
Marie Willoughby (16)   154

The Cedars School, Maidstone
Freddy Colaluca (13)   155
Lloyd Hatcher (12)   155
Michael Tsouri (14)   156
Adam Weston (12)   156
Toni Head (13)   157
Philip Hunt (13)   157

Townley Grammar School, Bexleyheath
Jodie Newland (12)   158

Villiers High School, Southall
Parminder Kaur Sahota (15)   159

Wilmington Grammar School for Girls, Dartford
Amy Liebthal (14)   160
Emily Allen (12)   161
Jessica Hibberd (12)   162
Laura Spitter (13)   162
Sharona Doyle (13)   163

The Poems

Home

In a land where it never snows,
The bodies lie by the thousands, where nobody goes
In the vast fields of dangerous mines,
Where the civilian and soldiers' lives entwine,
Where the palm trees are still swaying,
Thoughtless of the lives lost and still paying
The civilians' gentle hearts have hardened.
This harsh war will never be pardoned
But one day the war will end,
That is when the people's lives can be on the mend
And that is when the smiles will come out,
The people can start to run, jump and shout
And the people can once again be safe as can be,
Just like the waves that crash in the sea.
One day? Maybe . . .

Dayani Balasubramaniyem (15)

If I Were . . .

If I were an angel I'd watch over your head.
If I were God I'd watch over your bed.
If I were Santa I'd give you the Earth.
If I were a shepherd you'd have my mirth.
If I were a dog I'd let you ride on my back.
If I were a bird I would never attack.
But I don't need to be these things to show I care,
'Cause I have love and there's enough to share.

Victoria Elford (16)

The Precious Seasons

Spring causes plants to grow,
Tainted with a dark green glow.
The April showers bring rain
And cause the plants to flourish yet again.
The earth comes alive root first,
Then the buds, ready to burst.

The heat of the sun;
Scorching, ceaseless and intolerable,
Throws the plant into an impending state of doom,
However it blooms.

Autumn leaves auburn and brown,
Fall to the ground.
Yet through this carpet some green remains,
Because for some there is no change.

A harsh Arctic wind blows,
Bringing death along with its breath wherever it goes.
Life is left to fester and decay,
Jealousy has eaten it away.
The land is left barren and to waste,
Life has left with haste.

James Fitch (17)
Archbishop Tenison's CE School, Croydon

Jealousy

Jealousy is like poison swimming in your veins,
Causing that purple flush upon your cheek.
Jealousy is like an unexpected guest,
Which lingers, unwanted in your mind.
Jealousy is like a scorpion's sting,
A lash of pain as it tightens your heart.
Jealousy is like a faint whimper
But inside it's tearing you apart.

Jessica Holloway (17)
Archbishop Tenison's CE School, Croydon

Jealousy

There -
The bright light flickers -
But you ignore . . .

There -
Again it flickers,
A creature, darting -
But you ignore . . .

There -
In your ear -
But it's gone . . .

There -
In your ear,
A creature, humming -
But it's gone . . .

There -
The flickering,
The darting, the humming -
In the air, in your ears,
In your mind.
You cannot catch it,
You cannot escape it,
It hums, it darts, it fills your mind,
You twist, you turn, you flail your arms
But still it fills your mind -
A creature so small,
Humming,
Darting,
Filling your mind -
                    And it's gone . . .
                                There -

Pippa Line (17)
Archbishop Tenison's CE School, Croydon

Jealousy

Coarse, stark buildings crumble
Like icons brought to their knees,
The consequences of a resentful, watchful eye.
An ugly open space,
A gigantic fall.
The creation of a war-like state,
Built on the secret fears of a nation.
A country with something to fear,
Aggressive, determined.
The insecurity of a city,
Misunderstood, unnoticed,
Pride is fragile.
Its climate cold, hostile, prepared to engulf.
The first line of defence - easily overcome.
Citizens slaughtered, fade in destructive emotion
A resentful leader,
Insanely crazy.
Countries, buildings, cities torn apart,
Watchful, suspicious, guarded.
Is this caused by the protective edgy sensation?

Claire Harmer (17)
Archbishop Tenison's CE School, Croydon

I Am Who I Am

I looked at myself today not liking what I saw,
Every feeling that I have inside seems to be at war,
I close my eyes and open them again to see the pain I had before,
Feeling claustrophobic in a prison I call my heart,
I need to start to tear my views from others apart,
I've come to the conclusion to always say I can,
I'm stronger than I ever was when I first began,
If you object to what I say,
Never mind,
I am who I am,
Now and every day!

Jasmine Keating (13)
Archbishop Tenison's CE School, Croydon

Night In Our Eyes

Creeping, sleek, thin and fine:
A mere silhouette of the night,
Stalking the still streets
Its face hid from the light.
This creature hunts prey and corrodes from within,
Ensnaring its victim, tempting to sin.
Prowling the pavements with the dull patter of claws,
This beast claims lives and then silently withdraws
For its attack leaves no stain on the snow-white plain,
But burns at the soul, a smouldering fire to begin,
And as silently as the blood-red sun starts to rise,
So stealthily raises up its funeral pyre,
And as the golden rays break the night's ties
This creature's haunting face installs itself
In our eyes.

Christopher Tolley (17)
Archbishop Tenison's CE School, Croydon

The Waves

Silently I move in the night,
Without fear or fright.
I gently move with the breeze,
That is swishing in the trees.

I move the ocean's floor,
I swish onto the shore.
I feel the sun rise and
The warmth spreads over me.
That makes me feel glad that I am free.

The sun glistens over my blue waters
And gently I move in the sun.
I think to myself that nothing else matters
And that I am one.

Rosaleen MacCullagh (13)
Archbishop Tenison's CE School, Croydon

PE On A Rainy Day

Leaving the changing room nice and clean
Can't wait to start, everyone keen
Until we see the pouring rain.
I swear this could cause us tremendous pain,
Sleet, rain and hail throughout.
Shall I play football? Yes without a doubt.
The muddy ball whips you on the thigh,
I don't say a word but inside came a cry,
Hit by the ball on my numb frozen head,
Now I wish I was still in bed.
The slipping, the sliding, it's havoc over here,
The ball comes to me and I don't fear,
The touch to control and the pass away,
Why do we always have football on a rainy day?
Again comes the ball but this time I slip,
I hit the floor with the sound of a rip.
Your back flat on the icy, crispy grass,
If only I hadn't tried to make that pass.
I am muddy and in pain, drenched in my shirt,
The lesson now over and this time I've learnt
Bring an excuse for PE on a rainy day.

Kevin Silcock (13)
Archbishop Tenison's CE School, Croydon

Jealousy

The blazing red flickers from within,
Sparked alive by her treacherous sin.
It burns through my soul, my heart, decaying all trust,
Leaving only the thought of her bitter lust.
It runs through my blood fast and thick,
Waiting only for the hour's last tick.
Shadows engulf the daylight sky,
As darkness consumes my mind with her lie.

Lizzie Overton (17)
Archbishop Tenison's CE School, Croydon

Standing In The Rain

Can't you see my face?
Don't you feel my pain?
You can't see through my expression,
Well you'd better try again.

No one knows my problems,
No one really seems to care,
I feel if I were to die right now,
No one would be there.

I need you in my life,
Guiding me along my way,
You can't just leave me here
Standing in the rain.

You have to help me,
Stop me from thinking things I do,
Listen to my music,
That I have made for you.

Why do I feel as if I'm the only one here
And have nothing to gain?
Why am I so lonely?
Have you come to heal my pain?

No one can tell me why I'm so lonely,
You have not come to heal my pain,
All you do is leave me here
Standing in the rain.

Chrizzy Ecob (14)
Archbishop Tenison's CE School, Croydon

Jealousy

The dark green wax dries after the fiery light disappears,
The gentle husband's round face looks anxious and intense,
The soft, cream pillows laying on their bed
Matches the dearest wife's sleeping face,
He lays his body next to hers,
No sound is made,
He swallows deeply as he strokes her long black hair,
She jolts awake and his soft lips meet hers,
The hot, passionate relationship slowly coming to an end,
Thoughts rushing through his head - reminds him of a battlefield,
Unsure of his next move,
No more thinking, no more emotions, let it happen
He's telling himself as he clenches the pillow
That appears to have turned a charcoal-grey,
The gentle husband's round face looks anxious and intense,
The dark green wax is now completely dry,
As the noble Moor's love dies in his arms.

Philippa Bridger (17)
Archbishop Tenison's CE School, Croydon

Auschwitz

The sight of death's fumes score in the summit,
The stench of hopes and dreams trance the air,
Deprived bodies wander filthy dirt.

Yet hope still has its chance in few,
Those who clasp into freedom's rough hands,
These are the souls that savour life's every thought.

The image of hope deprives most,
For they all know it's just a dream amongst depressing thoughts,
Every minute is a life of terror.

Freedom,
Yeah.
Freedom,
Yeah right.

Joe Mott (14)
Archbishop Tenison's CE School, Croydon

I Am Midget

Who am I?
Or should it be what am I?
What is my name?
Why am I here on this Earth?
So many questions but still I see no answers.
I'll tell you who I am, tell you about my stupid body,
my stupid, stupid self.
I'll tell you what I am . . .
I am Midget, the child whom parents tell their children not to stare at.
Three foot tall, acne all over.
I am Midget the mess.
I am Midget, the small, young, frightened and able to do little
more than shake.
The disabled fool, who has a stupid dream of sailing.
I am Midget the mad.
I am Midget, who can't say my own name, or even count to ten.
I am Midget the mumbler.
I am Midget, who can't eat without dribbling, spitting or getting my
food all over myself and everyone else.
I am Midget the masher.
And yet I am Midget who has dreams like everyone else.
I am Midget, the fifteen-year-old that no one can understand.
I am Midget the misunderstood.
I am Midget, who can't read or write.
I am Midget the moron.
I am Midget, the unwanted little acne freak, the ugly little dwarf
that no one wanted.
I am Midget the mistake.
But most of all Dad knows, Seb knows, and I know.
Now also you know. You want to know who I am?
I am Midget the murderer.

I did it, I killed her, I killed her . . .

Micah Adams (14)
Archbishop Tenison's CE School, Croydon

Midget

This is me -
Smaller than a dream
Of owning a boat.

Smaller than a dream
Of sailing in the Ray Gut.

I shout and scream,
Can you hear me?
I am drawn to the water,
Drawn to the sea.

I am fighting fits,
Fighting taunts,
Fighting to eat my food,
Fighting Seb.

I smile but they laugh,
They don't see the world
As I do.

They don't feel the world
As I do.

Dad sees past my body,
All its deformity,
But he can't see past my brother's lies
And deceit.

This is me
Standing on my own two feet.

Ben Fixter (13)
Archbishop Tenison's CE School, Croydon

My Dream

I have a dream,
That I can sail away on the raging sea
And never return.
A place where I can step out of my skin,
A place where I can be me
And not what people want me to be.
I am like a snail trapped in my own shell
And when I step out
I'm a pathetic little boy,
With a grotesque smile.
I can't go anywhere alone,
I might have a fit and be left for hours,
No one to talk to,
No one to turn to,
Just me.
Puny little midget.
My brother picks on me
And I know why,
Because I killed my mother,
Midget the murderer.
My dad thinks Seb is perfect,
But he knows nothing,
I feel like I'm the mistake,
No one wants me.
Just because I can't speak doesn't mean I can't think,
People don't realise I have feelings,
They think I am useless junk,
Easy to throw away.
But someday they will see,
I have thoughts and feelings just like them,
They will soon be worried
And they will want me home.

Sarah Harger (13)
Archbishop Tenison's CE School, Croydon

Sailing Away

I hate my body, I constantly twitch and shake,
My body's covered with boils and spots,
Inside I shiver and quake.
I'm small, pathetic and weak
Like an ant that can be squashed,
Can't move, can't talk, can't even speak.

Shaking in my fearful room,
Swarming in the sea of enveloping darkness
Comes the echo of my worst nightmare, full of doom.
The malicious glare in his piercing eyes,
That threatening thrill in his voice,
What he says, is it truth or lies?

I know that gentle voice,
It sounds so loving, so kind, so soft,
He wants me to sail but I have no choice,
I'm mad Midget, too delicate, too small.
He's scared he might lose me like I'm a precious treasure,
He's scared I might slip, he's scared I might fall.

But there is a light in front of me,
A cloud of vision so clear,
Crystal clear, like the sea
And I will sail away
Through calm waters and crashing waves
So clear, I see this day.

Melissa Homer (13)
Archbishop Tenison's CE School, Croydon

Miracles In The Sea

I am locked in a room, no way out or in,
It stops me doing what I want to do
And it makes a difference between me and you,
I'm small and thin,
That's me, Midget, locked in my own skin.

Tormented in the night,
Threatened by my own brother
For 'killing his mother'.
Can't stand up for my right
Because I can't fight.

I shall sail my miracle man by day,
It was a deep, deep dream
But dreams come true, I have seen
In the harbour he shall lay
Till I come to sail it away.

Miracles are real,
They can be good or bad.
Inside me I feel
Those miracles can hurt or heal.

Nadine Richards (13)
Archbishop Tenison's CE School, Croydon

Jealousy

The familiar bitter tang,
The icy hand, a creeping cold sensation
With flashes of searing red,
Electric green,
A longing groan.
Dark, desperate clouds,
The driving rain
Bringing spiteful stabs of sour isolation -
This numbness is growing,
Overwhelming all other thought and feeling,
Creeping stealthily,
Slowly,
But surely
Into the open wound that is your heart.

Lucy Trueick (17)
Archbishop Tenison's CE School, Croydon

In The Dark We're All The Same

Black and white is what we are,
But somewhere,
There's got to be a bar.

Separated is what we are,
From harmony
We are so far.

But in the dark we're all the same,
That should come to you so very plain.

Why can't we all live happily
In the home we built?
Do you ever feel the guilt?

The KKK are an example for you,
You wanna be just like them too?

And read these lines very carefully:
In the dark we're all the same.

Sarah Khan (13)
Bentley Wood High School, Stanmore

Bravery Above And Beyond

I heard the call and had to go,
I never imagined what would unfold.
As I arrived, sadness filled my heart,
But I had a job to do, I had to start.
I with my friends ran towards the smoke,
Masks covering so not to choke.
In the building, up the stairs we ran,
Helping people down, giving them a hand.
Then the call came, the second building was hit,
But we had a job to do, we could not quit.
They said the building might fall
But we would never leave them all.
We continued up, to help those we could,
Not giving up doing our best as we should,
Then it happened, I saw it clear
A beautiful angel, holding her hand out near.
She guided us up, up above it all,
As we looked down and saw the building fall.
It was then we knew, our lives were gone,
But we mourned for the others, not our own.
Soon after the terror, our tears did fall,
Raining tears of sadness for it all
As our friends desperately search the site
Looking for small signs of hope and light.
Please do not mourn for us,
For we are in Heaven with Jesus.
Hold your head up high, and be proud of your land,
Stand together, hand in hand.

David Orrin (14)
Chatham House Grammar School, Ramsgate

The Sparkling Princess!

As he gazed into her eyes,
There he found a great surprise,
Her face said something he had never seen before,
Something so shocking he would faint to the floor.

She was so beautiful like a sparkling princess,
The look in her eyes like she had to confess,
But he didn't know what was her secret,
Or even know how to unleash it.

She had round, curved hips,
Smooth, kissable lips,
She was so fine,
Cute and divine.

Elegance would fill the air,
Something so magical you are left in despair,
Passion was always filling the air,
As long as she the beauty was there.

Her mouth was sealed she would never tell,
Only she would know the spell,
She was so beautiful jealousy took over,
Greed began to spread just like he told her.

He felt every beat of her pounding heart,
Every day it began to start,
Like a bubble ready to pop,
Would his feelings ever stop?

His love for her was one in a lifetime,
Constantly chills running down his spine,
She was so stunning it was love at first sight,
Anyone who saw her couldn't sleep at night.

Unless he was with her he wouldn't be alive,
Whenever she asked him he always denied,
Finally at last he did confess,
His love for his beauty, the sparkling princess!

George Florides (13)
Chatham House Grammar School, Ramsgate

Evil

His mind was pure and good at heart,
'Til something struck him and ripped him apart.
It screamed out inside him and tore up his soul
And where once was a heart laid a dark hole.

His eyes are red, menacing and cruel,
His skin is hairy, like that of a mule.
His clothes are torn and covered in blood,
His nails are rotten and covered in mud.

He takes his thrills from the sound of the victim's scream,
Whether it's cutting their throats or drowning them in a stream.
He's broken every commandment and completed every sin,
Everything about him is rotten like a bin.

Edward Teale (13)
Chatham House Grammar School, Ramsgate

Anger

The angered beast rampaged through the streets,
Knocking all over in its way,
It viciously munched on a fried chicken with one hand,
And swung a steel pipe around the other.
No one dared to approach him,
Otherwise the even worse angered beast inside with fury
Would break out.
Anger didn't care about anyone,
Just getting what he wanted,
Never to be questioned,
Or you might get a black eye,
For anger was quick with his fists,
But slow with his mind.

Lee Corfe (14)
Chatham House Grammar School, Ramsgate

Fear

Fear stalked his mind,
Fear stalked the ground,
Wherever he looked,
Fear circled around.

The pain grew worse,
It destroyed his throat,
Fear had moved on,
With no need to gloat.

Fear spotted a victim
Who happened to seem,
Happy and contented
And then came the scream.

Her head was left spinning,
Previously she'd felt fine,
But then she had felt
Like her life's on the line.

Fear had backed down,
But by no means was dead,
In his mouth he could taste
His victim's blood red.

Steven Rother (13)
Chatham House Grammar School, Ramsgate

Jealousy

Jealousy engulfed him like poisonous fumes,
Like a mummy about to climb out of its tomb.
It trapped him up like the gates of Hell,
As lust and envy rung his bell.
He yearned for everything, anyone owned
And sat by himself in his covetous zone.
He needed, he wanted, he had to have now
Like a farmer would yearn for his long-lost cow.
He sits in his circle alone from the earth,
Far from joy but so near to mirth.
So as he closes his coffin up tight,
His stench of jealousy floats into the night.

Emmanuel Donkor (13)
Chatham House Grammar School, Ramsgate

Bedtime

Bedtime is the time for peace.
Bedtime is the time to shut your eyes and go to sleep.
You keep your eyes shut really tight
And wait until morning light.
'Mum,' I called. 'I can't sleep.'
'Just close your eyes and try counting sheep.
I like to dream of something nice like riding on a motorbike.'
The windows were open, my curtains were blowing,
I ducked under my covers, there was something moving.
But it was only the shadows on the wall,
That nearly made me lose my cool.
And now I close my eyes to sleep
And try again to count the sheep.

Amy McGinness (11)
Dormers Wells High School, Southall

War And Peace

(For America And Iraq)

Where did this come from?
Why are we here?
Peace has run away
When we needed it.

America hates this community
They're having to live in.
Iraq has no food or water to live
But they die almost every minute.

Think, have a moment's silence
For those in danger and in emotion.
Have your say, war or peace?
Everyone wants peace, you just don't know it yet.

The war dungeon has returned.
Nobody can escape because
We've started World War III
In a world of war, no peace.

Jennifer Ingole (13)
Dormers Wells High School, Southall

My First Love

The first time I saw you
You made me wanna hold you.
The second time I saw you
You made me wanna like you.
The third time I saw you
You made me wanna love you.
The fourth time I saw you
You made me wanna marry you.

The fifth time I saw you
You made me wanna be with you.
The sixth time I saw you
You made me wanna die with you.

Tara McBeth (16)
Dormers Wells High School, Southall

Football Poem

The goalkeeper dived and made a save,
It was a valiant effort and it was very brave.

The players scored an excellent goal,
The crowds went mad and shouted, 'More!'

The player turned around and shot the ball,
But it hit the pole.

The player hit the ball, it went in the goal,
His name was Ruud van Nistelrooy,
The ball came off his sole.

As it was nearly over the opposition put in a tackle,
Out he ran fast as a jackal.

The Arsenal supporters shouted and went wild,
But Pieres slipped and on top of him Arsenal players piled.

It was over and Manchester United had won,
The fans went mad, the match had been fun.

Ibran Ahmed (13)
Dormers Wells High School, Southall

Someone Special

Is there someone you know that means a lot to you?
Well I do.
They are very special to me.
Without them I don't know where I'll be.
They are like a golden treasure.
They bring me so much pleasure.
Each day I think of them
And how much they mean to me.
When I think of them they take me into a deep dream.
Then I realise that we work better as a team.

Nickeisha Roberts (12)
Dormers Wells High School, Southall

Americans Invading Iraq

You go to liberate, then you invade,
Take away the peace and start air raids.
You kill the innocent and the guilty escape,
While your President sits at home with an earache.

You ruin millions of lives for the search of one,
When the looting started nothing was done.
You turn the happiness into rage,
Locked the innocent in a cage.

You came for the oil but you said you did not,
Let the rich escape and the poor rot.
You killed the people and left them in Hell,
You watched as the fire destroyed the oil wells.

You did not accomplish what you were looking for,
Spoilt the streets and let the fire roar.
Destroyed their city, left them with nothing,
And you left all the evil ones laughing.

Ryan Willmer (13)
Dormers Wells High School, Southall

My Little Sister

My little sister is sweet
But she can be annoying.
My little sister does bad things
And I get the blame.
I would take her to the shop
And she would ask for a lollipop.
My little sister will cry
And tell little lies.
Even though my sister's a pain
I will still love my little sister the same.

Shaniqua B Esprit (13)
Dormers Wells High School, Southall

I Wanna Be Yours
(In the style of John Cooper Clark)

Let me be your watch,
I will keep track of time.
Let me be your lotion,
I'll be your motions.
Let me be your moonlight,
To guide you at night.
Let me be your dream,
We will always be a team.
Let me be your star,
And may your life be a light.
Let me be your dictionary,
You can find the hidden words.
Let me be your love bird,
I will sing to you my love.
Let me be your teddy bear,
I will cuddle you so tight.
Let me be with you,
I'll love day and night.
Let me be your heart,
And we will never be apart!

Roma Givane (14)
Dormers Wells High School, Southall

Today, Tomorrow and Forever

Today the day flourishes with life,
Tomorrow the day subsides with life,
Forever cascading us eternally in time.
Today the day, an old love sparked my life,
Tomorrow the day we had uncontrollable feelings
For one another as life goes by,
But alas it wasn't meant to be,
As I didn't have the full commitment as he,
But soon he parted and I longed for his love,
And now I stand alone and wish on the stars above.

Amarjit Syan (14)
Dormers Wells High School, Southall

Peace

Why is there no peace on Earth?
Search for an answer inside you,
But I warn you,
You will never find it!

I'll tell you why.
If there was an answer,
Believe me,
We would have found it ages ago.

But I reckon there is a way!
And I bet you everything I've got,
It was always right inside you!
Of course,
The answer is *friends!*

Listen to me,
This fits for anyone in this whole wide world.
Though most of them wouldn't want to,
While most of us will.

Now the decision lies in your hand,
Hope you will turn it into a paradise land.

Janani Arulrajah (12)
Dormers Wells High School, Southall

A Friend Who Cares For You!

A friend is someone who's kind and cares for you.
If you're really a good friend you'll care for them too.
They make you smile and won't let you frown.
They always help you up when you're feeling down.
My mum's friend, she'll always love me,
She'll be there for me on a count of one, two, three.
You'll never wanna leave them, always and forever,
Because that's how a friendship grows.

Zahra Abbas (12)
Dormers Wells High School, Southall

It's A Jungle Out There

Cars roaring past like lions,
Their victims rushing out of the way.

People chatting away like monkeys,
With nothing better to do with their day.

Children like squabbling cubs,
Being impatient and rude.

Bins like vultures,
Scavenging left-over food.

Lamp posts like giraffes,
Heads up, up and away.

Wire fencing like tangled snakes
Keeping people at bay.

The road like one big worm,
Twisting and turning forever.

Motorbikes like leopards,
Staying quick clever.

Amar Singh Ruprah (11)
Dormers Wells High School, Southall

Love Poem

I can always come to you,
Only if you come to me.
I would love you all my life
If you never play me,
But if you wanted to dump me
Just feel free to tell me.
And I would never hurt you,
If you don't hurt me.
If you wanted to come back to me
You're free to call me.

Ibrahim Aden (11)
Dormers Wells High School, Southall

Sad Life

I don't know what it's worth to live,
Because this world has nothing to give.

Life isn't at all fair,
A perfect life is extremely rare.

In the streets people are always dying,
In the courts lawyers are lying.

In the shops it's very expensive,
Some shopkeepers are very offensive.

People are always lighting flammable things,
But you don't know if the fire brigade is a reliable thing.

Some police officers are very bad,
What this life has come to is very sad.

It's a hard life out there,
Put yourself first because no one else cares.

Roger Smith (11)
Dormers Wells High School, Southall

The Start Of True War

Picture yourself standing there
In the awkward silence,
No mother or father,
Nor sister or brother,
Just cold, dead bodies amongst you.

No tears left to cry
Or a voice to call for help.

Still the dust hangs there in the gloom,
You slowly grow cold just like them,
Night has come
But what can the new day bring?

Ceren Apaydin
Dormers Wells High School, Southall

Football

Football is the best sport,
Even though you have to go to the airport.
Thierry Henry is my favourite player,
He loves football and he is a real gainer.

David Beckham loves to score
But when he misses he loves to roar.
He is not very faithful
Because he moved to Real Madrid.

The best player was Ronaldo,
Then it got stolen by his teammate Figo.
Ronaldo is good at dribbling,
Figo was better at shooting.

Zinadine Zidane scores classics (goals),
But sometimes he hits the goalpost,
Sometimes he gives the keeper a lob,
That also makes him love his job.

Edwin Akoto (11)
Dormers Wells High School, Southall

Furious And Guilty

How furious I was, ready to hit and injure someone.
How upset I felt, as I am guilty.
I was ready to punch a lamp post.

Someone so loyal and so innocent
Has to go through the pain that I should be going through.
Oh how I wish I did not involve myself.

Now so upset, guilty and lonely
I walk through the town.
Every step I take my heart keeps telling me that I did the wrong thing.

But now so sad and so speechless
I walk down the road staring at the bars that I wished I were not in.
But now so sad and so guilty
I wish that I were that person suffering all that pain.

Jasmine Porter (12)
Dormers Wells High School, Southall

Chocolate

Chocolate, chocolate, chocolate
Is so nice and sweet,
It don't taste like wheat.
I have to have one to eat
Or I won't live another week.
Chocolate, chocolate, chocolate.

It's like another member of my family,
There is a whole variety.
I can't choose between them
'Cause I buy them all
Even though I'm small,
I won't be big and tall
I'll be short and fat like my neighbour's cat.
Chocolate, chocolate, chocolate.

I'm young and gonna die,
I don't want to be the one who lies
But I'm near the end of the line,
I ain't gonna be fine
So I won't be alive any longer,
The nurse said to be stronger
But my last words were
'Chocolate, chocolate, chocolate.'

Imran Shah (13)
Dormers Wells High School, Southall

Love!

When I first saw you,
I gave you a smile.
My teeth tingled
And my eyes sparkled in delight.
I was scared to declare my love for you,
I was scared to talk to you,
I was scared to kiss you,
But when I did,
I was scared to lose you.

Rubeena Pitchey (14)
Dormers Wells High School, Southall

Bridgette

You mean the world to me,
You are my best friend,
You beat me when necessary,
But our friendship always mends.

I'm dreading the day you die,
You cook the best shepherd's pie,
I forever need you in my life,
I'm so glad you're mine.

I love you more than anything,
I am your baby girl,
I feel relaxed when you sing,
You're worth more than diamonds and pearls.

You're an angel from above,
An angel sent from God,
You're really funny, you lend me money,
You're not only my best friend, you're my mummy!

Latoya Samantha Wilson (13)
Dormers Wells High School, Southall

Diwali

Diwali, the festival of light and forgiveness,
The day when the Lord Rama returned
After his 14 years of exile,
Lighted lanterns were placed for the Lord,
For his journey back home.

His return is celebrated by Hindus and Sikhs
All across the world,
With prayers, presents and fireworks.
Indian sweets are brought to share the joy,
The nice, sweet taste spreads the joy.

So come along
And join in with the fun,
Diwali only comes once a year.

Rakesh Gogna (14)
Dormers Wells High School, Southall

My Poem

I've never seen a monkey before,
Monkeys are funny animals,
Monkeys look up to me,
Their sense of smell is better than cannibals.
Monkeys tease people,
They climb trees,
This is not Shakespeare,
It's me.
I am a king to monkeys,
They adore me,
That's why I wrote about them,
They kick ass like Bruce Lee.
Why take animals fur?
Doing poems ain't my style,
They are innocent you know.
They have computers full of files,
Have you heard of King Kong?
My favourite kind of monkey are chimpanzees,
King Kong is the general,
They are like mini-mes.
This poem is bad,
There should be an NBA monkey team.
This poem is long,
Monkeys have a good talent, they should make a team.
Monkeys are crazy,
They smoke weed,
Have you seen them?
They eat seeds.
This is my rhythm
Hey! What's the time?

Bile Abdulle (12)
Dormers Wells High School, Southall

God Make My Life

God make my life a little light
Within the world to glow
To shine beneath the skies so bright
Wherever I may go.

God make my life a life full of peace
Within the world to share
To spread it all the spherical piece
Wherever I may near.

God make my life a love so rich
Within the world to spread
All the four corners of the Earth it reaches
Wherever it may be

God make my life a little shield
Within the world to guide
A little shield to all it yields
Wherever I may lie.

Temitayo Phillips (15)
Dormers Wells High School, Southall

My Sister

My sister walks in with her stylish hair
Chatting to me without a care.
She looks at me with a dirty stare,
My sister, my sister, my sister.

She says, 'Hello Aisha what's up?'
Standing there with my fancy cup.
My sister, my sister, my sister.

She walks off swinging her hips,
Turns around, she steps on my clips.
My sister, my sister, my sister.

There goes the tenth one,
'Oh dear,' she says, 'it has to be done.'
My sister, my sister, my sister.

Aisha Harris (12)
Dormers Wells High School, Southall

Today

Today I'm feeling bad,
Today I'm feeling sad,
What is making me feel so?
If only, if only I could know.

Sometimes I do feel a little sad
And sometimes I do feel a little bad.
But nothing compares to what I'm feeling today
'Cause today I feel bad in every way.

I don't mean to feel this mad
And also I don't mean to feel this bad.
I'm not doing it intentionally,
So won't someone come and rescue me?

So now that today I don't feel well,
I will be fine tomorrow, how can I tell?
It'll just be another miserable day at school
Where the kids'll pick on me cos they're cool
But I know it's not right, I'm no fool.

So for now I'll always feel bad
And I've no hope of ever being glad.

Mandy-Lee Boyd (13)
Dormers Wells High School, Southall

It Feels Good

Meeting you,
Talking to you,
I don't know how, why
Or what I should feel,
But it feels good,
I have known you forever
Till life ends,
But why I feel this way
I have no idea,
But it feels good.

Aissa Salimo (14)
Dormers Wells High School, Southall

What I Think Of Love!

For the sweetest guy around,
The guy I love, and who I've found.
You're special to me in every way,
Morning to night every day.
Thinking of you
Puts a smile on my face,
The person you are
I want never to change.
I wish me and you
Can last forever,
Until the end of time;
Nothing can break my love for you,
Because in my heart
You're mine.
I can live in a world
Where there's murderers around,
Who proudly hold up their chins;
But one world, I can never live in,
Is where my feelings for you
Are a sin.
You're with me now,
But in future where you'll be,
Even if it's far,
I hope your heart's with me.

Uzma Saleem (14)
Dormers Wells High School, Southall

Portrait Of A Madman

I whistle,
I laugh,
I tickle enough,
As strange as I am
I love butter and jam.
My hair is so messy,
My dress sense is wacky,
I love messiness and breadcrumbs,
I hate neatness and long nails,
My humour's unpredictable,
My style is indestructible,
They say I'm really mad
And that I'm just straight bad.
I say I'm happy, I'm free
And really, really healthy.
They said 'Here draw a portrait of yourself,'
So I wrote and wrote and wrote
But they didn't seem to be content,
So I wrote and wrote some more
But what I seemed to come up with
Displeased them even more.
I came up with my portrait
Of a madman careless and free!

Kancha Mbwengele (15)
Dormers Wells High School, Southall

The Snow Leopard

Through the ice clear snow,
There suddenly appeared a glow,
It was coming more and more towards me,
I saw a glow of white and black,
Suddenly I hear something tiptoeing on the ice,
Sh . . . sh . . .
There appeared a face,
It stared at me and the limits of its space,
I gazed at its space,
It was standing in the middle of the land it had
Surrounded by the Arctic Ocean.
It then sees its prey,
This lonely looking fish,
It then tries to catch it,
Then disappears, my guilty wish
As quickly as the lonely fish.
The lonely fish which turned about,
Flickered and moved towards the edge of land and into sea.
The leopard looked down on land,
It turned about thinking where shall I go?
I then put my hand out to give it a signal to come to me,
But it ran and went out like a fading light
Into the darkness, far from sight.
From sight, but never from mind,
Leaving its after-glow behind.

Namneet Preenie Gill (15)
Dormers Wells High School, Southall

She Who Waited

There she waited near the river,
Where she hoped she'd meet her lover,
Every day she'd do the same,
Sweetly calling out his name.
'Oh my darling come to me,
Don't just leave me here to be.'

She would sit and she would pray,
'Please come back to me some day.'
She'd look up high towards the moon,
Hoping her lover would come soon.
'Oh my darling come to me,
Don't just leave me here to be.'

It was with great sadness that she heard of
The tragic death of her only love.
'No, it can't be, it's not true,
For here I waited just for you!
Oh my darling come to me,
Don't just leave me here to be.'

Yet every day she went to the river
To remember her sweet lover.
'Remember how I called your name,
Remember how you never came.
Oh my darling come to me,
Don't just leave me here to be.'

For weeks and weeks she sat and cried
For her only love had suddenly died.
She couldn't stand these awful cries
And now deep in the river still she lies.

Charlene Badibanga (13)
Dormers Wells High School, Southall

Freedom

I am free to speak,
I am free to think,
I am free to go wherever I want,
I am free to support whoever I wish,
Freedom is a pleasing thing.

I am free to express what's on my mind
Without the fear of persecution.
Freedom is something we all deserve,
Yet for some, it's a distant dream.
I hope that one day
We all have the freedom we deserve
And regret the day
When it was a distant dream.

Harmeet Gill (13)
Dormers Wells High School, Southall

I Love You

I love you,
Yes I do.
You're so sweet,
Sweet enough to eat.
When I see your gorgeous face,
My heart begins to race.
I fancy you
For those things you do.
Your dark brown eyes
Make me realise
That I'm in love with you.
When you're with your friends you get so rude
And then I change my mood.

Stacey Moles (13)
Dormers Wells High School, Southall

Babysitting

I sit in a room listening for a cry.
The baby sleeps and I wait
To hear a cry and she will awake.

Many times before I babysat
But not a baby.
If she wakes she will hate me,
I'm afraid that she won't stop.

If I shout will she cry?
If I leave her will she cry?
If I lock her in her room
Will she cry the whole night long?

How long will she sleep?
Will she sleep through the night?
Will her parents come
And wish her goodnight?

Then she wakes and not a cry,
She drinks her bottle
And she lies on my lap.

Everything is great
And she doesn't even cry.

Charly Creagh (14)
Dormers Wells High School, Southall

The Things That Love Does

Love. What is love?
That is what I want to know.
Love is something that takes your heart
And squeezes everything out of it.

Love is not something that you nor I can hide, nor control.
It can come upon us at any time
And it cannot be shut away from the outside world.

Love is something that squeezes every drop
Of might into softness.

Once love is broken all that love will turn to
Anger and hatred.

Hatred will turn into pain, will turn into wounds,
Will turn into cuts and bruises.
Love is cutting me inside
And I am suffering in silence.

Saad Khan (14)
Dormers Wells High School, Southall

My School

School, school, school! Boring school!
At dinner time I play football
I don't like the classrooms, they are stifling hot
It's like I'm boiling in a cooking pot
My form teacher is so annoying
Whenever I see her I get a headache
I go into the canteen for lunch
And sit with my friends and munch and munch
Going to school makes me not feel cool
I would rather be swimming in a swimming pool.

Uljit Singh Sarna (15)
Dormers Wells High School, Southall

In My Dream

In my dream
I ate whipped cream.
I went to Mars,
On the way I ate some chocolate bars.

I landed on Mars
And saw flying cars.
In my dream
I saw a big green laser beam.

In my dream
I saw a football team.
I was putting on some cream,
I seem to be waking up.

In my dream
I saw a fire,
It was higher than the big tower,
it was started by a tyre,
That's what was in my dream.

Basharat Hussain (13)
Dormers Wells High School, Southall

Friends Forever

Hello, hello, my good old friend
I'll always remember you right till the end.

I can remember the day we said goodbye
When you got on the aeroplane to fly.
The way tears were dropping from each eye
I felt like I could die.

I'm sure we'll see each other soon
On the other side of the moon.
Last time I saw you I was only seven
Hopefully, good friend, I will see you in Heaven.

Chris Moles (13)
Dormers Wells High School, Southall

The Darkness

The dark, dreary night,
A star shining bright,
I hear a scream
Or is it a dream?
My heart beating like a clock,
My stomach churning like a key in a lock.

The dark, dreary night,
There is some light,
A candle burning,
A murder occurring,
A horse passing,
A person gasping.

On a dark, dreary night,
There is no light,
Something happens
To anyone, anywhere,
The darkness is screaming,
And it's soon to be light.

Dimple Gohil (15)
Dormers Wells High School, Southall

Friends Or Not?

I'm going to give my heart to you,
Because love is true and so are you,
And then you give yours to me,
So everyone can see our friendship is for eternity!

I'm here for you,
But the question is are you there for me?
So please don't betray me,
Because we were made to be!

Of all my friends I've ever met,
You're the one I won't forget,
Because God's in Heaven and above,
And you're the one I'll always love!

Rajwant Cheema (14)
Dormers Wells High School, Southall

Come To The Caribbean!

Come to the Caribbean, where the food is luscious
Collect all the seashells and make them your precious
Visit all the sights and the Pitons too
Take a look at the Cathedral; it's older than you
Swim in our warm clear waters and seas
Have all the honey you want, even talk to the bees
Our volcano has been dormant for years and years
All the movies we make fill your eyes with tears

Come to the Caribbean where you can be you
Have a great tan or maybe even a tattoo
Greet all the neighbours and feel welcome here
The crickets make noises, they're wonderful to hear
Visit the Sulphur Springs and our museums too
I'm sure they'll have valuables in store for you
Go on a nature walk and climb the hills
Be whatever you want to be, express how you feel

Take a trip round the island and eat all the food
Make sure you have a bite, I'm sure it tastes good
Drink all the drinks you'll like to have
Eat all the puddings, we don't want you to starve
Sleep peacefully at night, wake up fresh in the morning
Enjoy the rest of the day, especially the evenings
Come to the Caribbean and tell all your friends
When you go back home, I'm sure you'll come again.

Patrish Lionel (14)
Dormers Wells High School, Southall

The Staffroom

What lurks behind the staffroom door?
I bet you want to know.
Is it nice or nasty? No one's really sure
It's where kids can never go.

Is it a gym
Or is it a disco?
Can my teacher do a backflip?
I'd really like to know.

I know they eat and drink in there
I've heard them laugh and chat
They go when they've got time to spare
My friends and I know that.

Maybe it's dark and full of gloom
Do they keep a scary creature?
How can I see that mystery room
I'll have to become a teacher!

Serena El-Kurd (12)
Dormers Wells High School, Southall

Robert Pires

(This poem is dedicated to Robert Pires, the man of my heart)

R avishing
O nly one of him
B eautiful smile
E very day he appears in my heart
T errific skills

P ainful job
I nteresting thoughts
R ainy tears
E verything I could leave for him
S ome day he'll be mine.

Haleema Yousfzai (11)
Dormers Wells High School, Southall

Friendship Just Ain't What I Want!

What does friendship mean to me?
Something that just isn't meant to be.

Tired of this, I've had enough.
Tired of pretending this isn't love.

But you want a friendship, that's a fact.
That's what makes me want to crack.

We're the stars that shine so bright,.
We only come out on a magical night.

I know that love is in your heart,
So why are we spending so much time apart?

My love is your only hate.
Will you decide if this is fate?

Why isn't this friendship love?

Chorin Kawa (13)
Dormers Wells High School, Southall

Perfect Love

Love is a feeling no one can explain
But if anyone falls in love, you know the one to blame.
The one to blame is the perfect one.
The one with beautiful hair and that good-looking bum!
I can't stand perfect loves
They are so, so perfect!

I think they are not worth it,
Wasting time thinking about them.
Wasting time worrying about them.
Just fly away,
Live like a dove.
There is no point
For love!

Hado Mahamed Omer (13)
Dormers Wells High School, Southall

It's The War

It's already happened,
It was all so sudden.
The tomahawk missiles,
Went through the sky,
Hearing their whistles.

Poor, brave young men,
All hiding in their pens.
Bang! Off goes a bomb,
Possibly another tom.
Why do we do it? There is no point.

Bush and Blair,
Act as a pair,
Having talks that don't even matter,
Yet the battle just goes on clattering.
Why do we do it? There is no point.

Saddam Hussein is in hiding,
Doing all his biding.
Firing missiles at our men,
As they go running into their pens.
Why do we do it? There is no point.

Biological and chemical,
Both very dangerous.
All can die in just one blow.
Both shouldn't be used, yet they are.
Why do we do it? There is no point.

Darren Ward-Bain (15)
Dormers Wells High School, Southall

A Mixed-Up World

I sat at my table at a quarter to three,
I drank up my cupcake and ate up my tea.

I buttered my coffee,
Put milk on my toast,
My slipper chewed the dog then moved onto the post.

I wound up the cat and let out the clock,
I pulled on my shoes and laced up my socks.

I taught my teachers a lesson or two,
About how to stick paper and how to cut glue.

I drove home on foot,
It was a bumpy ride,
I felt really happy so I cried and cried.

It was warm and snowy
So I wrapped up cold,
And retold a story that I'd never told.

This is the poem you've never seen and will never see again
And trying to make sense of it will make you half-insane!

Stephanie Murray (13)
Dormers Wells High School, Southall

What's The Meaning Of Family?

Family are always there for you
they always help you through
any difficult times,
not loving you to them is a crime.

They give you love that no one else can
you can trust them like a solemn vow.
They never let you down
and never let you frown.

This is the meaning of 'family'.

Syrah Ghoier (14)
Dormers Wells High School, Southall

The One

I saw this pretty girl in Hollywood
she had green hair but she was looking good
she made me fly
when I saw her thigh
she was so pretty
and this girl
was as precious as a pearl
I fell in love
like a dove
I asked her out
she slapped my face
I felt like a disgrace
I hated life
I wished I had a knife
to stab myself
and die
to never have lived
but she came and apologised
and she kissed me
and I lived happily forever
with her
together!

Arsalan Abtahi (12)
Dormers Wells High School, Southall

When I Go To The Park

When I go to the park
I see squirrels gathering nuts, then they run off without a trace.
When I walk around, I see birds taking food to feed their young.
I hide or the rabbit will see me as it burrows into its hole.
Conkers fall to the ground from the trees' branches.
The leaves fall, waiting for autumn.
The wind attacks, swirling them away.
When they go, I go away.
Swishing and swirling away.

Paris Mandalia (13)
Dormers Wells High School, Southall

Grandma's Necklace

If only you were here to see it all
I hold it like a treasure
It's always beside me
I'll never let it go
Because it's so lovely
Back then you handed it over
And now you have passed away
So now day after day
I just sit and say,
'I wish you were here, you meant the world to me,
Now that you've gone and left me.
If only you were here
I could see you one last time
And tell you that I love you
And that I feel blue without you.
If only you were here, we could have bonded more.
If only you were here to see it all!'

Massara Hassan (11)
Dormers Wells High School, Southall

The Life Ends

The lifetime ends
Your time passes
Some people go shopping for the trends
Spend your lifetime on an adventure
Girls and boys beat people up for revenge.

Don't sit around and yawn
Just go on an adventure
Straight after you are born
Jump up and down, enjoy the fresh air
Don't sit down and yawn, yawn, yawn.

Patricia Ann Ward-Bain (12)
Dormers Wells High School, Southall

Only In A Year

Once more it starts again,
From when the spring flowers blossom
To when the winter snow arrives,
And in-between them,
The golden sun
And the crispy autumn leaves.
It's all in a year.
Only a year.

Once more it starts again,
From the great dilemmas we face,
To all the sacrifices we make,
And in-between them,
All the problems in life attack us,
And all the surprises emerge for us,
It's all in a year.
Only a year.

Tamana Darwish (12)
Dormers Wells High School, Southall

Friends

Good friends are those *who help* without hesitation,
Who tolerate without frustration,
Who remember without limitation,
And *who care* even without communication!

As precious as you're to me,
As precious as no one else can ever be,
I know all friends are hard to choose
But only you would be hard to lose.

If kisses were water, I would give you the sea.
If hugs were leaves, I would give you a tree.
If love was a planet I would give you the galaxy
And friendship is life, I will give you mine for *free!*

Sahar Wahedi (11)
Dormers Wells High School, Southall

Nature's World

As I look out the classroom window
the trees are still as gold
I turn around and they're rustling like an angry hippo.

I go to the zoo, look at a lion,
he looks charmingly at me,
then turns round roaring at me angrily.

I feed the horses with bright yellow hay
they smile at me then I turn away
turn back round, they try to jump at me
so I just walk away.

I go to bed, nice and warm
my mum comes in and brings me some milk
I close my eyes, hear a noise
I don't know what it is, I hope it is just my toys.

Courtney Payne (11)
Dormers Wells High School, Southall

Have You Got A Real Friend?

A real friend is one who walks in when the world walks out.

A real friend is someone who is there when he or she
would rather be somewhere else.

A real friend is someone who knows the song in your heart
and can sing it back to you when you forget the words.

A real friend is a person who know all about you
and still likes you.

Friendship:

Don't walk in front of them, they may not follow.
Don't walk behind them, they may not lead.
Walk beside them and prove to them that you are a real friend.

Sambridi Gurung (11)
Dormers Wells High School, Southall

Winter

Winter has come and summer is gone,
Children want to play all day long,
But their parents won't let them go
To play in the snow.
Children like to play a game,
When the snow came.

Children are good,
When they are eating food.
Snowflakes are all different shapes and sizes,
Some snowflakes are shaped like stars.
At night, snowflakes fall down like rain,
Snow everywhere, up on the roof, out in the garden, everywhere.

When the weather is good,
Parents let children out to play in the snow.
Children have fun and they build a snowman,
They throw snow on their friends and have fun.
Dancing, playing, singing, having fun,
When the snow comes down.

Birds sing with joy,
'What a lovely day,' they say.
Birds play in the snow,
And they sing to show their happiness.
Birds have lots of fun,
They fly up high in the sky.

Winter is more fun than summer,
Having fun in the snow.
I like winter because of snow,
And wish for it every day.
Winter is cold and snowflakes fall down.
Winter is lots of fun that we can enjoy.

Joyla Merly Da Cunha (12)
Dormers Wells High School, Southall

Nature

Flowers are nice
Flowers love water
There are many different flowers
But which are its daughters?
Bluebells ring
Like school bells
Daisies love the water
Birds sing
While church bells ring
Teachers shout
While Brussels sprout
Doors open
While hearts are broken
Love is a mystery
(That rhymes with history)!

Elisha Russell (12)
Dormers Wells High School, Southall

Snake

S lithery snake looks for prey,
L ike a radar detecting an enemy,
I n the hot and gloomy sand of the desert.
T hrough the desert going 20 miles per hour,
H earing and detecting everything.
E ven after eating, still hungry for more.
R aging in to eat its prey.
Y ear after year, growing like a beast.

S lightly coloured in the dark.
N ever sleeping but always on the lookout.
A n attention-seeker.
K nife-like teeth ready to chew meat.
E nough is enough, the tired snake rests after a day's work.

Sunny Gogna (12)
Dormers Wells High School, Southall

I Am A Cheetah

I am a cheetah
I run very fast
I am a cheetah
I run like a bullet
I am a cheetah
I like to eat meat
I am a cheetah
I have brown spots
I am a cheetah
I have a yellow body
I am a cheetah
I have sharp teeth
I am a cheetah
I live in the jungle
I am a cheetah.

Dany Fayed (13)
Dormers Wells High School, Southall

My Teacher

A person who is important to us.
A person who we need a lot.
A person who is like our parents.
A person who I love.
A person who likes us.
A person who teaches us the knowledge of life.
A person who shows us the right way to know knowledge.
A person, a person, a person.
A person who I love.
A person who I need.
A person who likes us.
There is no other person you can find
It is just my teacher
          who is so kind!

Awista Siddiqi (12)
Dormers Wells High School, Southall

Spain

The summer of Spain is boiling and hot,
So when you're walking outside you can enjoy what you've got,
But to live in Spain, it is very, very different,
Because it's hot all the time and you've got to be very confident.
To cool off when you're outside,
Go for a walk or go for a ride,
So when you come back you feel soothed,
And you can get on with your work in a good mood.
At night you sleep and feel much better in the morning,
So you can get up to scratch with your work and stop dawdling.

Amandeep Saini (11)
Dormers Wells High School, Southall

That Someone

That someone's voice I hear in the morning.
That someone who makes me mad.
That someone I love and care for.
That someone who makes me sad.
That someone who makes me angry.
That someone who makes me a man.
That someone who keeps me up all day.
That someone who says I can.

Akash Kumar (11)
Dormers Wells High School, Southall

Autumn

Autumn is here at last.
The golden bushy leaves.
Mushy, bushy leaves, to kick all the way.
Nice as gold, yellow as flames, red as blood.
Sunny as orange, dancing around me in the howling wind.
My black shiny hair is dancing too.
It's time to say goodbye!

Imaan Raza (12)
Dormers Wells High School, Southall

The Seasons

Spring
The first day of spring is cool,
I feel like relaxing like a fool.

In spring the flowers bloom,
They're almost as big as a balloon.

Summer
A summer's day is when it's nice and sunny,
That's when the bees make their honey.

Autumn
Autumn is a season when things cool down,
That's when the children have frowns.

Autumn is when there are lots of conkers,
That's when children drive their mums bonkers.

Winter
Winter has days when it's freezing,
That's when people are sneezing.

Winter is full of snow fights,
That's when it's low in Fahrenheit.

These are the seasons, what can I say?
The seasons are priceless, no one can pay.

Doran Halliday (11)
Dormers Wells High School, Scuthall

Carriage Of Death

Plants waving in sorrow over the silent body
Sunbathing in death
A distraught boy, his mouth open in grief
As he loses a part of his soul.

Daniel Boulton (13)
Downside Middle School, Newport, Isle of Wight

Dusty Roads

Petrified villagers running for their lives down the beaten paths
Smoke polluting the daytime air
The stench of cooking rations
Deafening shrieks of anger, fright and despair echoing
down the street!
Who knows what awaits them further down the road
As you hear the bomb sirens screech out over the town?
Bellowing gunshots
Flying aeroplanes
Knowing they're your enemy.

These people's lives will never be the same!

Jordan McLuckie (12)
Downside Middle School, Newport, Isle of Wight

The War Boy

A booted-up boy
Mindless of what lies ahead
Endless shadows of boy in war.

A mine on belt
About to be used
In a matter of days
He could be dead.

James Fahy (13)
Downside Middle School, Newport, Isle of Wight

The Endless Fight

Petrified villagers running down the dusty road for their lives,
Smoke polluting the air,
Terrified children sprinting from the soldiers,
Deafening noise they hear in their ears,
Who knows what will happen to the emotional people?

Matthew Wadmore (13)
Downside Middle School, Newport, Isle of Wight

Soldiers

Terrified children running from soldiers
Deafening shrieks caused by soldiers
Dust flying up from the boots of soldiers
Chased out to be shot by the hounding soldiers
Screaming children running from war
A soldier's drill pounding the houses
From the shots of the soldiers
Victims on the floor
Dying!

Olly Crook (12)
Downside Middle School, Newport, Isle of Wight

The Unwanted Truck

One corpse lying silently on her deathbed,
The distraught child losing a part of his soul,
Sunbathing in death.
Her brother's face drooped in painful grief,
Her erased face
Makes the boy think,
What's left of the human race?

Harry Hemming (12)
Downside Middle School, Newport, Isle of Wight

My Golden Angel

My heart is sprinting, swimming, skipping,
Your eyes shine in the shimmering sun,
You have hair like the golden desert,
My love jives on the seafront,
You are a peaceful rose in the flower bed,
My love is dancing inside me.

Timothy Peek (12)
Downside Middle School, Newport, Isle of Wight

War!

Everyone's scared
But nobody's giving up,
Determined to win . . .
It's such a sin,
But nobody's giving up.

Children crying . . .
People dying . . .
Bombs keep dropping -
No one is stopping,
The aeroplanes keep flying.

Guns keep loading . . .
Soldiers keep walking . . .
Bullets keep striking -
Enemies keep going down.

In the end we forget why we started,
Innocent lives being hurt or worse -
dying . . . !

Vicky Lowe (12)
Downside Middle School, Newport, Isle of Wight

Too Scared To Feel Pain

Burnt from head to toe,
Hand waiting to be held,
Arms outstretched like a bird waiting to take off.

The bloodstained bed and bandages,
Blotched and stained with blood,
Ruined knees, never to walk again.

All of the doctors feel disgrace
Such a thing could happen,
Hanging on to life by a support machine,
War, war, war, will be the end of us all!

Jade Dove (12)
Downside Middle School, Newport, Isle of Wight

Hanging On For Life

Like a bird waiting to fly,
His outstretched arm, feeling for a hand,
Too scared to feel the pain,
Hanging on for life.

A bandaged mess,
Covered in burns,
Ruined knees, knowing he will never walk.
Hanging on for life.

Blinded eyes for evermore,
Alone in a dark world,
He feels no more pain,
There is too much light,
He couldn't hang on any longer!

Katie Brookes (12)
Downside Middle School, Newport, Isle of Wight

An Unhappy Life

Rushing, shouting, banging,
Everyone's alert.
People bringing bad news, panting,
Children scurrying, covered in dirt.

Mother in deep sorrow
For her dear husband and son.
Waiting . . .
For more chaos?
Only for her son.
Clasped hands and fearful eyes
Betray her torture.

Hannah Windley (13)
Downside Middle School, Newport, Isle of Wight

Devastation

War.
As the bombs silently drop,
And the bullets ricochet into the distance,
Brave men fight for their country,
Saving the injured villagers.

War.
As the dead stare them onward,
The soldiers break into a run,
And as the bullets shower the trenches,
All men fall from standing.

War.
Then suddenly comes a blinding light,
Like the sun has collided with the Earth,
As everything is burnt into the hells of the world,
There is no victory
For anyone.
Just devastation.

Stuart Collins (12)
Downside Middle School, Newport, Isle of Wight

Life's Not Fair

Lying silently,
She had done no wrong,
Her brother distraught,
His mouth drooping in disbelief,
With an erased face,
As she sunbathes in death,
Her brother losing a part of his soul,
And with plants waving in sorrow,
There she lies, peaceful!

Martin McDonough (13)
Downside Middle School, Newport, Isle of Wight

There, There, Dead And Gone

Here, there, bang and gone!
There, there, bang and gone!
Bloodstained walls
And children crying
In a second
Dead and dying!
There, here, bang and gone!
Here, here, bang and gone!
With black smoke
You start to run
Far away
Away and gone!
Here, there, bang and gone!
There, there, bang and gone!
No one left
You're alone
Run for your life
Run, yes, run!
There, here, bang and gone!
Here, here, bang and gone!
Engulfed in smoke
Flames around you
Swim in death
And death around you
Here, there, bang and gone!
There, there, dead and gone!

Ben Reay (12)
Downside Middle School, Newport, Isle of Wight

The News

The news, like a black smog, suffocating and cruel
The news, like a dark angel leading them to the truth
The news, only cruel words to those awaiting theirs
The news, like a key unlocking bears.
The news, maybe you'll hear yours soon.

Anthony Wallace (12)
Downside Middle School, Newport, Isle of Wight

My Family

My mum is fun
My mum is great
She lets me go to bed later
Than half-past eight.

My dad is super
My dad is playful
My dad is better than the rest.

My brother is mad
He can be sad like a bunny
And he's not funny.

My sister is happy
Because she is alive
God has put her on this Earth
To decorate it.

Jack Mackins (11)
Hartsdown Technology College, Margate

The Wind Is . . .

The wind is a howling wolf
Waiting patiently for a juicy meal to come past
It's late at night for a deer to walk past.

The wind is a bee
Whispering through the tree, going from plant to plant.

The wind is an owl
Spreading his enormous wings silently making a cold draught.

The wind is a tiger
Flickering in the flames waiting for a meal to come by.

The wind is a squirrel
Carrying dandelion seeds along, picking up crackling nuts.

Cara Mei Kember (12)
Hartsdown Technology College, Margate

Winter

One of the seasons I like best is winter
Wrap up warm in your scarf and vest
Do some jobs to earn some cash
Take your dog for a walk
Whilst skidding on the ice.

Summer's here now
It's nice and warm now
No need to wrap up warm now.

Lauren Callaghan (11)
Hartsdown Technology College, Margate

My Secret Box
(Based on 'Magic Box' by Kit Wright)

In my secret box I will put . . .
The twinkle dart of my heart
A photo of all my family playing
The timing of the sea
The washing of the waves
The sound of children
The last leaf of an old apple tree.

Fairlie Ward (11)
Hartsdown Technology College, Margate

Cat In The Kitchen

She sits on the window sill, sunbathing all day
And when she's ready, she gets up for a drink
Her fur is soft as silk
Her eyes sparkle in the moonlight
She's the queen of the kitchen.

Lucy Foster (11)
Hartsdown Technology College, Margate

Life

Why are we punished?
Life can be such a heavy burden,
Why is there war?
We are punished
But what for?

What comes after life?
Is it but a test?
Why do we suffer for other people's mistakes?
Bombs and weapons are made to blow living things to dust,
People killing God's most precious gift, life,
Destroying the home He gave us.

People starve, people die,
Why, oh, why?
Life is like a time bomb ready to go, any minute, any second,
We only have a certain matter of time,
So make the most of it.

For the dark cloud is cast over the world,
Where is the sun?
Where is the light?
Where is the world's hope?

Bradley Thompson (13)
Hartsdown Technology College, Margate

Family

Family is someone who takes care of you when you're ill
Family is someone who listens to you when you have problems
Family is someone who makes you happy when you're sad
Family is someone who plays board games with you when
it rains outside.

Christina Skillen (11)
Hartsdown Technology College, Margate

Scared

When I'm scared I hide
And hope that no one will find
Or anyone will see
Any trace of me

I keep very quiet
Despite all my fear
I clench every part of me
And hope no one can hear

I'm also scared of the dark
But hide under my duvet
I say, 'Don't worry,' to myself
And await the day

But I hope that when I'm older
This fear will come to an end
I won't have to worry anymore
I'll have lots of friends!

Jasmine Ayles (11)
Hartsdown Technology College, Margate

Winter

Winter and Christmas are closing in fast.
The trees, covered in snow,
Start to shiver and blow in the wind.
The houses start to twinkle in the darkness.
Parents in a rush to buy presents.

Christmas is here
And you can feel the excitement in the house.
We run downstairs to see the sparkling presents.

It's New Year's Eve and Christmas decorations come down.
The excitement is over.
We will have to wait until next year.

David Sims (11)
Hartsdown Technology College, Margate

Old Age

As children go to school
Eyes trapped in houses like cages
Watching them frolicking
Remembering the day they could play.

Venturing out, shuffling along,
Spending the day shopping for company,
Inexpensive,
Remembering the day they had family and friends.

When people look at them, thinking
Please don't let me go like that
Looking in the mirror
Remembering the day when they were beautiful.

When they get too old for families
They become castaways
In a world full of strangers
Remembering the day we respected our elders.

Ben Turner (13)
Hartsdown Technology College, Margate

Old Age

Autumn is the ripeness of life
Leaves wrapping around it
Fading away, suddenly, it's winter
Winter is the darkness of life.
The leaves wrinkling up
The wind dying down
Suddenly it gets colder
The eye in the sky dies
It gets dark
Soon she sleeps forever
Never to wake up.

Darren Wynne (13)
Hartsdown Technology College, Margate

The Old Age Poem

It reminds me of the sun
One minute it's shining bright
Then suddenly it is night.

It reminds me of an apple
One minute it is ripe and colourful
Then suddenly it's wrinkly and ready to pass on.

It reminds me of a fish
All its life it fights to get upstream
And then it dies after fulfilling its duty in life.

It reminds me of a tree
It starts from a seed
Then it grows into an enormous, beautiful plant
Then it slowly dies away
From people chopping the tree down bit by bit.

Benjamin Mason (13)
Hartsdown Technology College, Margate

Old Age

Old people are like autumn,
Birds migrating while old people hide from the cold,
Hibernation takes place,
Harvest finally arrives,
Leaves turn different colours,
Weather changing,
Winter is upon us,
The trees are all bare,
Old people live for a long time,
Until their time's up.

Sophie Healy (13)
Hartsdown Technology College, Margate

My Cat

(For Perrins, my special kitty)

My cat is white and brown
He jumps upside down
You'll never see a frown
When my kitty's in town

When he climbs out the window
Onto the roof
I hope and pray
That he doesn't spoof

When he climbs on the landing
On that top hall
He keeps me hanging
For I hope he won't fall

My cat is the greatest
My cat is the best
But when he falls over
We all laugh in jest

My cat is crazy
He's round the bend
But I love my cat
He's my best friend.

Sean Hampton (12)
Hartsdown Technology College, Margate

Fashion

Fashion is a hard thing to keep up with,
But that's the way you have to live,
If you want to keep in with the crew,
That's what you have to do,
There's always someone who's the best,
From new trainers, to a new vest,
If you're not fashionable enough,
Life begins to get tough.

Katie Chelton (12)
Hartsdown Technology College, Margate

Hamster Poem

Oh hamster, hamster, you are so sweet,
You keep your cage so very neat.
You stuff your cheeks with lots of food,
Your table manners are quite rude.
You like to swing and hang from bars,
When you sleep you see the stars.
You like to run around the wheel,
And make it move and squeal and squeal.
Sometimes when we leave the school,
You escape in the dead of night,
Giving us an awful fright.
We follow the paper trail,
Your escape plans always fail.
We find you chewing books,
Giving us guilty looks.
In your nest you look so sweet,
Nice to hug and soft to touch.
Nibbling on a hamster treat,
Fudge, we love you very much.

Sian Vizzard (11)
Hartsdown Technology College, Margate

Old Age

It's a part of life
When it comes to an end
When you get wrinkles and start to shrink
And your back starts to bend.

It means you get grey hair just like mist and fog
Those little grannies sitting in their wheelchairs
Remembering how they used to jog.

It's nearly time to die
So have a rest and say 'Goodbye.'

Alisha Thornett (13)
Hartsdown Technology College, Margate

My Horse

My horse
He jumped a course,
He is really fast
He is never last,
He cannot stand still
He is never ill,
He is quite old
But he's never cold,
He's very frisky
And he's a bit risky,
He likes to be fed
When he's in his bed,
He lets others ride him
When I'm beside him,
His name is Torrie
But he does not like lorries,
He's not very sorry
When he does not load in a lorry,
His trick is to give you a kiss
Which he does not miss,
I like the animals,
They are mammals.

Charlene Welsh (11)
Hartsdown Technology College, Margate

A World Of Peace

A world of peace is true
No more war or frights
No bullying or calling names
A world of peace is what we need.

Daniel Dean (11)
Hartsdown Technology College, Margate

Dogs

Dogs can be big or they can be small,
They can be short or they can be tall,
Like a Great Dane, a Staff or a poodle,
If you want a dog for a pet,
Here is a choice of what you can get,
A collie, a bulldog or a Scottish deer hound,
Here are some more that I have found,
A greyhound, a dachshund or a bloodhound,
You can sponsor a dog for only a pound,
Just pay a pound a week if you start now,
A whippet, a pointer or a chow-chow,
If you want a dog just gather around,
I suppose you could have a basset hound,
A Dalmatian, a German shepherd or a Labrador,
And if you don't want one, it's me to ignore.

Melissa Hamer (12)
Hartsdown Technology College, Margate

Old Age

Old age is like a tree
It starts from a seed
And then grows
Then grows leaves

In the middle of its life
It starts dying
The branches start to die.

But when the branches
And leaves die
The tree is dead!

Jamie Daniel (13)
Hartsdown Technology College, Margate

Christmas Tree

C hristmas tree,
H olly leaves,
R eindeer are flying,
I vory on the door,
S anta giving out presents,
T insel wrapped around trees,
M erry Christmas,
A ngels blessing people,
S inging carols.

T ree in the corner,
R udolph is happy,
E ntertainment all around,
E xcitement for everybody.

Jason Williams (11)
Hartsdown Technology College, Margate

My Parents Are Aliens

My parents are aliens, they have to be
They have one long tail as you can see

And don't forget the two antennae on their heads
And the shredded skin on their beds

They talk gibberish in each other's ear
Though what they say I cannot hear

Maybe they're dressing up for Hallowe'en
Hopefully they haven't been seen

My parents are aliens, they have to be
No they're not - silly me!

Emily Wonford (12)
Hartsdown Technology College, Margate

Great Grandad Poem

This poem is about my great grandad.
Grandad, you died five years ago,
I can't believe it, is it so?
I know you were very old,
You were always so bold.
You served in the Second World War,
I know you felt proud to the core.
We always had so much fun,
Larking about in the sun.
I know you really loved Nan,
I got embarrassed when you sang.
I know you thought a lot of Chris,
And the same about Nan's sis.
I didn't know you for a very long time,
I still don't know if you liked lime.
We always used to mess about,
I remember, when we sang, 'I'm a little teapot short and stout'
I remember when we moved to Milton Keynes,
I still don't really like beans.
This poem is about my great grandad.
I love you Grandad very much.

Rebekah Tumber (12)
Hartsdown Technology College, Margate

Old Age

Old age
Old age
What is old age?
Is it just a number
Or a life stage?
What is old age?
When you get wrinkles
Or false teeth?
Good grief!
When you retire, what a relief!

Lauren Lipscomb (13)
Hartsdown Technology College, Margate

The Thief Lord

Did you hear about the thief?
He only nicked beef
When he went to steal
He would come back with a hefty bill
One day when he went to sea
He met the amazing me
We walked and talked along the prom
'Surprise' - out popped Dom
The three of us
Got hit by a bus
The thief and I got up
The thief got bitten by a pup
I went to the pub
Ordered a lovely plate of grub
I went back home
Just to be alone
I retreated to my room
Returned armed with a broom
I said to Mum
'You've got a big bum'
Mum gave me a whack
So I decided not to come back
This is the end of my tale
About time I was back on the trail.

Chris David Pannell (12)
Hartsdown Technology College, Margate

Animals

Some are big, others are small,
Some are tiny, some are tall,
Some are hairy, others are bald,
Some can be cuddled, others you can't hold,
Some are wild, some are tame,
Not all animals are the same.

Siobhan Pretty (11)
Hartsdown Technology College, Margate

The Haunted House

Stairs are creaking,
Tap leaking,
Witches moaning,
Ghosts groaning,
Lightning flashing,
Thunder clapping,
Curtains flapping,
Candles glowing,
Shadows growing,
Guns shooting,
Owls hooting,
I've got to get out of here!
The ghosts are coming near!
The door is open, out I run,
Out into the midday sun!

Laura Palmer (12)
Hartsdown Technology College, Margate

Old Age

The autumn winds came rushing in,
From across the hills they lingered there
And touched her hair.

She walked with me
All forlorn
She sang her song
And then we walked,
Those crispy leaves amongst our feet,
My gran and me
The autumn breeze.

Nicholas Carrington (13)
Hartsdown Technology College, Margate

Football Crazy

I want to play football
Even though I'm a girl
I am still quite good
So I'm writing to tell . . .

I put on my boots
And picked up the ball
And knocked for my friends
And told them all.

I picked the teams
We kicked the ball
We wanted to win
Said us all.

The game kicked off
On the centre spot
I ran down the middle
And took on the lot.

In front of the goal
With the keeper to beat
I blasted the winner
Right under his feet.

The whistle blows
It's the end of the game
We come off the pitch
And they're chanting my name.

Leigh Page (12)
Hartsdown Technology College, Margate

Animals

Monkeys, monkeys all around,
Up in trees or on the ground,
Little babies holding tight,
They go to sleep at night,
They sleep on branches, they sleep on leaves,
They eat fruit and are very bad with bees,
Some of them are huge, some of them are small,
Some of them are really cute,
And some just aren't at all.

Turtles, turtles in the sea,
Swimming softly in Hawaii,
Turtles with wired shapes on their shells,
Like big, beautiful, brown or green bells,
Brilliant swimming skills,
Like the navy seals,
They grow and grow as big as can be,
Little babies swim slow and easily,
They swim very well
As you can tell.

Whales, whales are fish,
That don't fit on a dish,
They are fat,
They're not scared of bats,
They are the best at swimming,
And do a lot of fishing,
They swim so far,
You cannot catch them up in a car.

Deni Arklie (11)
Hartsdown Technology College, Margate

Silly Dan

Silly Dan was a stupid man
He drove a 2cv
He was so stupid, more stupid than even me
He was an engineer, he was fired for breaking a gear
When he got home his friend was near
And offered him a sweet or two
But he crossed the road and off came his shoe
Into a puddle of mud
Poor Dan's leg was then covered in sludge
But his friend asked him for a lovely bag of fudge
As he walked in, he wiped his feet on the mat
But then was tripped over by the stupid, fat, black cat
As he got up he went to the flat
To take off some fat
But then fell out of the window
And caused a bit of a show.

Simon Watts (12)
Hartsdown Technology College, Margate

All About Me

Alex is my name
Leaping for fame
Lentils are the worst
They make me want to burst
Always lending a hand
For every grain of sand
Opening the door
For every man on shore
Tea please!
Or I'll throw away the keys
And that's all about *me!*

Alex Moore (11)
Hartsdown Technology College, Margate

Animals

I have a dog
I have a cat
My auntie Sophia has a bat
She takes it here
She takes it there
She takes her bat everywhere
I had a spider
I have a rat
Well, we did till I got my cat
My auntie Sophia's bat just sat
Until my grandad came home with a hat
I had a snake
I had a monkey
That's until it called the bird, 'Chunky'
That's when we got rid of the monkey
Then we got a lion
What a beast
He ate my brother for a midnight feast
Then we got rid of all the animals
Instead we got a little mouse
We left it alone and it wrecked the house
It ran away, the little mouse
It still now walks round the house.

Hannah Taylor (12)
Hartsdown Technology College, Margate

The ABC Of Animals

A is for an angry alligator
B is for a bashful bird
C is for a crazy cat
D is for a dumpy dog
E is for an enormous elephant
F is for a funky fish
G is for a giggling guinea pig
H is for a horrified horse
I is for an ignorant iguana
J is for a jolly jaguar
K is for a kind kangaroo
L is for a lazy lion
M is for a magic mouse
N is for a naughty newt
O is for an odd octopus
P is for a precious piranha
Q is for a quiet quail
R is for a raging rabbit
S is for a slithering snake
T is for a tamed tiger
U is for an unseen unicorn
V is for a vicious viper
W is for a wishful whale
X is for my 'xcellent poem
Y is for a yakking yak
Z is for a zippy zebra.

Katie Brown (12)
Hartsdown Technology College, Margate

Animals Are Great

Animals are great.
Never mistreat them.
I love animals, I have eleven.
My animals are all different.
All animals are great.
Lots of people don't think like this.
Some people just mistreat them.

All animals deserve some love.
Right or wrong, what do you think?
Everybody loves an animal.

Giraffes are big.
Robins are small.
Every animal is great.
Any animal is special.
To love an animal is great.

Samantha May (12)
Hartsdown Technology College, Margate

Changes

Winter's coming
Summer's going
Everyone is cold.

Summer's gone away
New schools for some
Scarves, hats and coats,
Can you see it is freezing for me?

Come on, let's play
Let's build a snowman
We can find some buttons for him
Cool, let's play.

Jessica Gadsden (11)
Hartsdown Technology College, Margate

Football-Mad

Football is good,
Football is bad,

Football is fun,
Football is sad,

I play at school
And with my friends,

I take a free kick,
Oh, look how it bends!

My friends laugh and joke,
So I give them a poke.

That was my poem,
What a good joke!

Matthew Richardson (12)
Hartsdown Technology College, Margate

In This World

In this world
There're lots of things happening
But what are we to do?
We have no power
Or say in the world
But we do have an opinion
We may not be able to speak up and tell anyone
But we can think and dream
Of the power we could have
Maybe some day we could have power
And help people in need.

Bethany Wigley (13)
Hartsdown Technology College, Margate

A Little Frog

There was a little frog
Who sat upon a log right in the middle of the lake
With pop-out eyes and great big thighs
He would sit and eat the flies
He would eat and eat and stare at his feet
Until all the light was gone
When it was dark he would have a lark
And sing his favourite song.

Jade Jewell (11)
Hartsdown Technology College, Margate

Zoom

My grandma's dog, Zoom, looks cute and sweet,
He sits and begs for a treat,
He always chews electrical wires,
And barks at people who are walking by us,
He digs up mud on the lawn,
And we find the tissue paper has been torn,
But I don't care what he does as such,
Cos I love him very much.

Rebecca Stevens (11)
Hartsdown Technology College, Margate

Happiness

Happiness is bright pink,
It tastes of white chocolate,
It smells of flowers,
Happiness looks like presents at Christmas time,
The sound of music in my ears,
Happiness is a soft, plump cushion!

Rebecca Lawrence (13)
Hartsdown Technology College, Margate

I'll Be There

Although you may not love me,
Although you may not care,
If ever you should need me,
You know that I'll be there.

Your heart may be broken,
Your love may not be free,
But when your heart is broken,
You can always count on me.

I'll never stop loving you,
I know because I've tried,
All the oceans couldn't hold,
The tears that I have cried.

Adam Chapman (12)
Hartsdown Technology College, Margate

Old People's Poem

Old people are pale and weak,
Some old people groan when they speak.
Old people are like clouds with their wrinkly faces,
Most men and women can't keep up a fast pace.
Old people live for a very long time,
Just like they are never going to die.
An old person is an old dusty table,
And an old person is a bony skeleton.
Grannies' voices are usually croaky,
And most of the time they like to pinch and poke you.
An old person is an autumn tree,
Leaves go down,
And leaves turn brown.

Talos Williams (13)
Hartsdown Technology College, Margate

The Rat Boy

There was once a boy,
Who was only half a rat,
Because he was scared of his pet cat.

When he went to school, the children laughed,
And used to shout out 'Look!'
He ran to the library where he felt safe,
But the kids put the tail in the book.

When the rat boy got home,
He started to cry,
And ran to hide in the cupboard,
His parents said, 'Oh why? Oh why? Oh why?'

The rat boy came out,
And wiped away a tear,
He said, 'I have no friends,
And I know that they are near.'

'But who are they?' his parents said,
'They are the kids in my class.'
Then the rat boy went
And said, 'I really hate my class!'

He went to school and stood up to them,
'For you are so very wrong,
And when I have lots of friends,
You won't be laughing for long!'

Hannah Young (12)
Hartsdown Technology College, Margate

In The Forces

I'm leaving today,
I'm going far away, to join the army,
My mum has made me a cake,
I will eat it slow,
Because I know it will be the last cake I see.

I'm at the barracks,
I wave goodbye
And see my mum begin to cry.

I'm in the dorm unpacking my stuff,
The others arrive
And they look chuffed,
The sergeant comes in,
And looks at us,
He said, 'A haircut is a must!'

We are on the assault course,
To see if we are fit for the force,
I only hope I can do the trials,
My body aches after just ten miles,
The ramps are high, the logs are cold,
I almost slipped on the mould.
I can see the finish, what a relief,
My body is giving me so much grief.

A shower, then some food,
What a first day as an army dude!

Mark Roberts (12)
Hartsdown Technology College, Margate

Attractions

Wouldn't it be wonderful if we could only see,
the Leaning Tower of Pisa leaning over me?

Wouldn't it be wonderful if we could only see,
the Great Wall of China standing 6-feet over me?

Wouldn't it be wonderful if we could only see,
the Grand Canyon dipping miles under me?

Wouldn't it be wonderful if we could only see
The Tower of London's deserted prisons haunting me?

Wouldn't it be wonderful if we could only see,
the Great Barrier Reef's tropical fish staring up at me?

Wouldn't it wonderful if we could only see,
all these places around the world and see them all for free?

Zoe Heavey (12)
Hartsdown Technology College, Margate

Ice

Ice on trees makes you shiver inside,
Icicles as sharp as shiny as a knife in the sun,
Wrap up warm for the day ahead,
Put on the fire and rest in bed,

The next day is bright and full of ice,
People skidding around,
Oh, how nice!

Robert Mason (11)
Hartsdown Technology College, Margate

Invicta

There's a school called Invicta
It's definitely the best
It's really a great school
It's better than the rest.

The teachers are nice
The hallways are clean
It's like a beautiful swimming pool
Filled with chlorine.

In the library the books are arranged
In a special way
I always take a book
Nearly every single day.

If you're home in bed and sick
And you're hoping to get better
They'll send you some homework
If you write them a letter.

If you have missed
They will assist
For Invicta's the best
Better than the rest.

Jasmine Jakubowski (11)
Invicta Grammar School for Girls, Maidstone

Happiness

Behind a winter's dark day,
Tiny dreams whisper and play.

Imagine a time when you are warm,
Safe inside far from the storm.

Think of things that made you glad,
Don't dwell on times when you were sad.

Believe in wonder and never forget,
This life is for living and not for regret.

Samantha Woolley (11)
Invicta Grammar School for Girls, Maidstone

School

School can be quite boring,
Sitting around all day,
You usually end up snoring,
Until it's time to play.

Art is quite exciting,
DT's quite cool too,
English is lots of writing,
Maths is lots to do.

Registration very hasty,
Science very taxing,
Lunch is very tasty,
Form time quite relaxing.

Home time, home time, fusses, fusses,
We are going home,
People trying to catch their buses.
In their house they'll roam,

Homework is quite tiring,
Raking your brain for answers,
We only end up perspiring,
We'd rather be tap dancers,

Now it comes to end our day,
Off we go to bed, 'Wahey!'

Clara Metcalfe (11)
Invicta Grammar School for Girls, Maidstone

Winter Fun

The snow lies silently on the ground
Footprints appear without a sound
The mice curl up to keep themselves warm
Hiding away from the bleak, icy storm

The trees shake off the layers of snow
The smiley face of the sun doesn't show
The children run round having snow fights
While parents relax enjoying the sights

Landscapes cuddle under their white rugs
While grandparents shiver and sip out of mugs
The snowman smiles as he has made a friend
But understands that his life will soon end

As the snow goes gradually overnight
The snowman knows that he is right
The children excitedly run out to play
But realise their fun has gone away!

Katie Wood (12)
Invicta Grammar School for Girls, Maidstone

Dolphins

D olphins leap and dance at sea,
O ver the beaming, orange sun,
L earning from the older ones,
P ractise makes you that much better.
H iding all their best talents,
I n their underwater worlds,
N eath the land of strange people,
S wimming in the depths.

Amy Kemp (11)
Invicta Grammar School for Girls, Maidstone

The Sun Comes Up

The sun comes up when the morning dusks
The sun goes down when the evening dawns
Bright and early we wake up
And see the dew upon our lawns.
When night-time comes we go to bed
And feast our eyes upon the stars
Then suddenly the moon appears
And following behind comes Mars
Then once again the sun comes up
Its beams shine brightly down to Earth
And all the children go to school . . .
. . . The sun shines on the Astro Turf!
After school the children leave
They climb onto the bus
The bus drives round and then it stops
The children come home safely to us.

Jorjia Croucher (11)
Invicta Grammar School for Girls, Maidstone

A Poem

The beautiful bright sky
Stands proudly on high
Clouds flowing softly in it
The sun keeps it lit
When it is dark at night
The moon shines in delight
White stars start to glow
The wind begins to blow
Now it is late
I want to contemplate
My day that I've had
So . . .
Goodnight!

Francesca North (11)
Invicta Grammar School for Girls, Maidstone

The Sea

The sea is a hungry dog,
Pounding upon helpless boats.
Swallowing whole ships,
Claiming the lives of unknown sailors.
'Bones, bones, bones,' he mutters,
Crunching loudly.
A smug smile curling its way across his face.
He leaps! Crashes! Against the white chalky cliffs,
Gnawing at the soft stone.

Yet on calmer days,
Come midsummer,
A playful puppy runs up and down the sands,
Rolling around in the long grassy dunes,
Lying beneath the beating sun,
Softly dreaming.
Nothing can arouse him,
But the faint taste of . . . bones . . . bones . . . *bones!*

Alix Rowe (11)
Invicta Grammar School for Girls, Maidstone

What Lurks Behind You?

Shadows creep up on you,
as you wander through the night.
Turning through the alleyways,
they know how to keep out of sight.
The stars are shining brightly,
causing more shadows to appear.
When a movement sounds behind you,
and you feel a sudden chill of fear!
So when you dare to turn around,
are you surprised to find,
a massive pair of jaws,
begin to bind?

Kelly Inman (11)
Invicta Grammar School for Girls, Maidstone

Sweet Seasons

The sweet Summer party of brightness
Fades away slowly as Autumn comes in, in a fallen leaves dress
She brings with her a dusty breeze
Which blows Summer away until she falls on her knees

As the sun of Summer has gone, everything dies
The leaves fall down like flies
They make a carpet for the majesty of Autumn
As she enters with her fellow friend, Wind,
Who makes everyone's fingers numb.

As Wind makes the trees shiver and lose their final leaves
Autumn laughs as she hears Summer's grieves
Ice swept nature later on like a bird's wing flapping
By surprise Winter comes in early, leaving Autumn gawping

The leaves get covered by a bed of snow
As the Queen enters and all the people like us they know.
Know that Winter brings Christmas with presents
Presents for the children who are really quite pleasant

Zooming by, Santa flies with presents overflowing
Christmas lights embedded in snow start glowing
But soon the fun is over and done
So out comes for Spring, the sun

Bursting with glory, the leaves and the flowers grow back
The bulbs are then planted out of a sack
The bulbs sprout to begin a new year
Nature celebrates with a big cheer

Marigolds, pansies, daffodils and tulips
The bulbs grow like this with stems and flowers on their tips
Trees grow new leaves for fresh starts
New branches grow like darts

The new year is always colourful
So everyone is cheerful.

Charlotte Friend (11)
Invicta Grammar School for Girls, Maidstone

Ode To Shopping

Shoes and tops, lots of shops
I'll buy and buy until I drop
Spending money is so great
I think shopping is my fate!

Getting ready for a shopping spree
I love shopping and shopping loves me
Mobile, money, coolest clothes
In my pocket, they're burning holes!

Calling my mates,
Making a date
For a big shopping trip
All my mates say that I'm really hip!

Well, they wouldn't be wrong there, would they?

Emily Mayhew (11)
Invicta Grammar School for Girls, Maidstone

Winter

I love the winter
I love to snow fight
It's warm and cosy
On a winter night.

I love making snowmen
With black blobby eyes
But when the sun shines
The snowman sadly dies.

I love the fluffy clouds
They make me want to stare
It might be raw and cold
But I don't really care.

Saira Ahmed (11)
Invicta Grammar School for Girls, Maidstone

Little Monsters

I know people say,
Little monsters only come out at day.
But I have proof for you,
My very own eyes have seen it!
I wouldn't like to repeat it.
Before I tell you the horror
I would like to say,
Anyone with a weak constitution should
stay away from the subject.

Little monsters come in all shapes and sizes.
They like to prank and play
And argue every day!
They act as good as gold,
But I know what they behold!

I can't tell you anymore,
The effects could be permanent
So next time you see a little person
Run away,
Don't stay!

Alice Whittaker (11)
Invicta Grammar School for Girls, Maidstone

Summer

S ummer is hot, nice and bright,
U nder the blazing sun,
M eals outside with buzzing bees,
M illipedes and flies,
E nd of the day, time for bed, sleeping on the covers,
R ise and shine, another hot day to be outside in the air.

Holly Saunders (12)
Invicta Grammar School for Girls, Maidstone

Dead Grandad Experience

Curtains drawn,
Lights on,
TV on,
Voices, voices,
Shadows, shadows,
Black, black,
Can't see,
Help, help!
Ghost, ghost,
Spirits, spirits,
Dazzled, dazzled,
Not me, not me,
'How are you?'
Silence, silence,
Wind, wind,
Wish, wish,
Utter, utter,
'Grandad . . .'
'My child'
Scared, scared,
Stiff, stiff,
Awakening the dead?
Dreaming the dead?
Viewing the dead?
It can't be . . . Grandad?

Lauren Elphick (11)
Invicta Grammar School for Girls, Maidstone

You Shall Never Get Bored Of The Rings

L ord of the Rings is thrilling for all
O ne ring will possess Frodo at the Witch-king's call
R uthless Gollum decides Sam and Frodo's fate
D eath for them, he'll get the ring, he can hardly wait.

O ne Fellowship will save the world from Sauron's evil grasp
F or elves and men shall join again to defeat him, that's their task.

T alent of archery is Legolas' game
H orseback riding will bring Aragorn fame
E xceptional is Gimli who is rather small

R iders of Rohan are very tall
I n Helm's Deep black is the sky
N ot prepared to be attacked by the Uruk-hai
G reat army of 10,000 against 1,000 men,
S o many lives lost, shall Gondor rule again?

Selina Towers (11)
Invicta Grammar School for Girls, Maidstone

The Fox Hunt

They sit there every day and night,
Paralysed with nerves and fright.
Tears are hidden in their beaming eyes
And then a terrifying huge surprise . . .
The sound of hooves, deep breath, a scary shout,
The noises fill the air about.
And then a vicious scratch, bark, tear,
Red water everywhere,
A life is wasted once again,
An animal taken from his cosy den,
A life so short,
Just for a sport,
That's not fair,
Imagine if you were there!

Poppy Partridge (11)
Invicta Grammar School for Girls, Maidstone

Hallowe'en

Hallowe'en is my favourite night,
I love giving the children a great big fright.
What shall I wear
That will have a great scare?
Maybe a black hat,
With a big fat cat.
But what about my wig?
I hope it's not too big.
With a long black curl,
It will make people hurl.
Big fat warts and a horrible long nose,
People will stare, when at the door I pose.
Around my body I could wear a cape,
People would look with their mouths agape.
With our goodies and tricks up our sleeves,
What we could do, you wouldn't believe!
Hopefully, 'treat' will be said first,
Otherwise you'll end up being cursed.
At the end of the night,
All children are tucked up tight.
All the ghosts and witches will disappear,
But never fear, we will be back next year.

Rebecca Abbott (11)
Invicta Grammar School for Girls, Maidstone

My Brother

A happy face,
A beaming smile,
That cute little nose,
Those puppy dog eyes,
He's the cutest sweetest bubba I know,
And that's because he's my baby bro!

Georgina Owen (11)
Invicta Grammar School for Girls, Maidstone

The Weasel

Slim and swift creeping through the night.
Climbing over walls, feather-light.
A small bundle clutched in her jaws.
Running and leaping, diving on all fours.

An owl hoots, a farmer raises his gun,
Animals frightened, start to run.
Dashing, hiding, running quick,
Give no evidence, not a snapped stick.
The bundle moves, squeaking in fright.
The mother reassures her, holding her tight.

Over crops, dashing away.
Got to survive till the next day.
A mouse runs out, she resists its thrall,
Focusing on the hound dog's call.
A huge stone's standing tall,
A challenge for a creature so small.
She scrambles up, breathing fast.
She's risking her life and it won't be the last.
Over and over she climbs walls, gates and fences.
Trying to find her den with all her senses.
And there at last her burrowed hole home.
Safe and sound where she is free to roam.

Rhian Stone (11)
Invicta Grammar School for Girls, Maidstone

Flowers

Flowers, flowers, on the ground,
As pretty as can be,
Flowers never make a sound,
Covered with humming bees!
Purple, yellow, blue and green,
All that you have seen,
So be careful with these loving things,
And be careful with these loving things!

Hannah Turner (11)
Invicta Grammar School for Girls, Maidstone

My Valentine

I do like you,
I think you like me too,
The only thing is,
I don't know how to kiss!
We could just talk,
Or go for a walk.

Please don't laugh,
Otherwise my heart will break in half,
We could go out,
You might be in doubt,
About my mum and dad,
They'll let me out for a tad!

I'm writing this poem, to let you know,
I do like you, I think we flow.
The only thing is,
I don't know how to kiss!
So for today you are my valentine,
Please can you be mine?

Leah Roberts (11)
Invicta Grammar School for Girls, Maidstone

My Animals

I have an animal that lives in the garden,
She is very rude but at least she says, 'Pardon.'
She is called Ruby, although she is not red,
But she is a good girl and goes to bed.
Her sister, on the other hand, is good all day long,
But I do have to wake her up in the morning with a big loud *dong*.
They were born on Valentine's Day,
Soon after they came to stay,
Came to stay with me,
Of course they were jumping with glee.
My guinea pigs, that's what I call them, my guinea pigs.

Rosie Gouldsworthy (11)
Invicta Grammar School for Girls, Maidstone

My Night-Time

When I lie in my bed at night,
I think, I wonder,
What's wrong with me?
Why can't I sleep?
I think back to what happened today,
What happened at school,
It was an ordinary day,
Nothing much,
I think what was on television earlier,
There wasn't anything on that was good,
Nothing much,
I think what dreams that I've had on recent nights,
I didn't dream though,
I can't go to sleep . . .

Charlotte Sheppard (11)
Invicta Grammar School for Girls, Maidstone

Inspiration

My teacher told me to write a sonnet,
But I really don't know what to put on it.
I thought I'd write a poem instead,
So many things came into my head.

Trees, flowers, chocolates galore,
War, world peace, humanity and more.
I can't get any inspiration in this classroom,
It fills me with nothing but darkness and gloom.

I feel nothing special, I feel nothing sad,
I feel nothing good, I feel nothing bad.
And here I am still thinking away
There's nothing in my poem yet and I haven't got all day!

Rhiannon Prosser (11)
Invicta Grammar School for Girls, Maidstone

A Poem About Love

What is this thing,
This feeling called love?
A natural thing from the stars above.
It makes you smile, you sing for a while,
After you've found your own love.
Love is wonderful, a beautiful thing,
You always end up with a dazzling ring
From the man who makes you smile!
You're sure to be with him for a while!
So who is your valentine crush?
I bet if I guess him, you will blush!
But that is a good thing, I assure you of that,
Keep it a secret tucked under your hat!
I have my own which I'm not going to tell,
But you will find out when there is a wedding bell!

Claire Street (11)
Invicta Grammar School for Girls, Maidstone

Daydreams

Every day I wake up to see,
A big yellow face smiling down at me.
I sit in bed and think of the dream,
A galloping horse or a running stream.

Sometimes I dream of how the world works,
How the wind blows and how the shadows lurk.
But suddenly I'm woken by a teacher's shout,
'Maddy, what are you dreaming about?'

I sit up and stare around the room,
It looks like a big pit of doom!
A teacher's red face,
Looking at me in disgrace.

Now I look up panic-stricken,
what's about to happen makes me sicken!

Madeleine Starks (11)
Invicta Grammar School for Girls, Maidstone

Wake Up

Your eyes are almost dead
Can't get out of bed
And you can't sleep.
You're sitting down to dress
And you are a mess
You look in the mirror
You look in your eyes
Then you realise
Everybody goes
Leaving those
Who fall behind!
Hang on
Though we try
It's gone!
Did I smile?
Did I cry?
Just before I said goodbye.

Natasha Johnson (11)
Invicta Grammar School for Girls, Maidstone

My Nature Poem

Nature is such a wonderful thing,
It's quiet, peaceful and pretty,
There are flowers and birds that sing and sing,
It's the opposite of the city.

It's not noisy and it's not loud,
In fact it is almost silent,
And without it, the world we know,
Would be very violent.

Kerry Cheeseman (11)
Invicta Grammar School for Girls, Maidstone

Winter

I woke up early one morning,
Just as the crow started cawing,
And saw a glittering blanket of snow!
Before long my snowman had started to grow.
Wrapped up all warm,
It doesn't matter if my clothes get torn!
My nose is red, my cheeks are pink,
My hands are blue and my feet are starting to sink!
Christmas Eve and spirits are high,
There's never even a heavy sigh.
Christmas Day and everyone's lined up outside
the front room door,
All waiting to see the presents scattered all over the floor!
The oozing, dripping, succulent turkey, with the crunchy
roast potatoes,
Throwing the leftovers out for the crows.
Now Christmas is over and New Year is near.
Time for us to look forward to the start of the New Year.

Bethany Lucas (11)
Invicta Grammar School for Girls, Maidstone

Hallowe'en

Hallowe'en is a scary night
Although the bats don't often bite
Lizards watch you while you sleep
Leaping frogs give you the creeps
On the way you're not alone
We're following you all the way home
Eels waiting in your bath tub
Eerie lions wait for their cubs
Never will you be alone.

Megan Libbeter (11)
Invicta Grammar School for Girls, Maidstone

Tiger For Tea

I once invited a tiger, to come round for some tea,
He rang the doorbell with his paw and was more polite than me,
I was not scared, oh no not me, for I'm so very brave,
When I asked him where he lived, he replied, 'A cage.'

I told him to keep quiet, because Mummy was asleep,
He nodded his head and promised not to make a peep.

'Would you like some food?' I said,
He replied, 'Yes. Then I should go to bed.'
I offered him some ham but he told me, 'No.'
'Beef, fish, what would you like?' I asked the tiger who was now
                                                            lying low.

'Oh, I don't know, I'll just have something nice.'
'Sweets, chocolate, ice cream or would you like some mice?'

So I raided the big, white fridge,
It was becoming quite a squidge,
Boxes, tins, cans and packets were everywhere,
Tiger sat licking his hair.

'Oh, forget the food, would you like a drink?'
'Yes,' he said, as he walked across the cans that had started to sink,
He turned his head, 'It's OK, I don't need a map.'
When he got to the bowl, he stuck his head under the tap.
'Don't do that, you'll drown!
Oh why do you turn all my food down?'
'The truth is,' he said, 'I'm a veggie, I don't eat meat,
But come to think of it, you look rather sweet!'
Chomp, chomp, chomp, chew, chew, chew!

Tiger bit my leg in two!

Charlotte Adamson (11)
Invicta Grammar School for Girls, Maidstone

My Auntie

She's going to be fine,
she really is.
Just believe in God and
give her a kiss.
Give her a hug,
put faith in her heart.
Wake up in the mornings
and pray in the dark.
Go visit her and give loving gifts.
Make her happy and faithful,
all she needs is one big loving kiss.
She's not alone, not at all,
she's got all her friends and family to call.

With love to my auntie, all will go well.

Lauren Billington (11)
Invicta Grammar School for Girls, Maidstone

The Sunset

Yellows, reds, pinks and blues, fill the sky like wondrous news.
Swirling patterns in the sky, a lovely effect as the swallows fly by.
I sit on a hill and lie on my back as the night grows darker,
I pack up my bag
And head off down the old mud track.
In the morning when the sunset's gone down,
The rosebuds open as I set foot on the ground.
I'm looking forward to a brand new day,
Another friend and a place to play.
As another day has passed me by, I glance up at the welcoming sky.
The clouds are getting ready to move away,
And the lights are going down to prepare for another one of those
spectacular displays.

Holly Louise Froud (11)
Invicta Grammar School for Girls, Maidstone

Trick Or Treat?

Hallowe'en the dreaded scare
For parents and OAPs, it's not fair
When they go and make some toast
Who turns up? A devil and a ghost!
They ring the doorbell to demand some sweets
The people in the house don't make a peep
The bowl of treats is sitting there
But nobody wants to have a scare
'Trick or treat?' the phantoms cry
Lightning flashes across the sky
Through the darkness they see a face
Making their hearts stop, then race
The door flies open with a smack
Goodness me, it's Uncle Jack!

Georgina Haynes (12)
Invicta Grammar School for Girls, Maidstone

From The Back Of The Room

Felt so sad but yet happy,
Couldn't believe my friends were around me,
Fiddling around with unfinished homework,
Ever so educated but just so disorganised.

By watching them close, I can see,
What's their personality.
Most running around making paper planes,
Not thinking about what life will bring.

But what I learn most from sitting alone,
Is most people would rather be at home,
When children in poverty wish for a school,
We're all here, not grateful at all.

Michelle Thompson (11)
Invicta Grammar School for Girls, Maidstone

Me

I can't write poems easily,
I find them really hard,
Bear with me,
I'm writing this in my backyard.

I go to school from nine till three,
I listen, learn and play,
My favourite subject is PE,
I enjoy the day.

My favourite sport is netball,
My uniform was blue,
I represented my old school,
We didn't ever lose.

In my world I have friends,
Who dance and play with me,
This will never ever end,
As far as I can see.

In my spare time,
I go to Guides,
We salute our special sign,
And play games inside.

Georgina Evans (11)
Invicta Grammar School for Girls, Maidstone

Your First Day At School

When you are five, on your first day at school,
Everyone seems so big, when you are so small,
Your teacher is friendly, the first thing she'll say,
Is 'Off you go, children, go off and play,
Play with the water, play with the sand.'
'That's hard what you're drawing, dear, shall I give you a hand?'
You play with the water, you dig in the sand,
You draw a nice picture, you shake Miss's hand,
You have fun and play, until the bell goes,
What happens now, nobody knows.
You get stuck in the crowds, you get pushed to the hall,
Oh no, you've heard the scary headmaster's call!
You're so scared, you squeal and run,
This isn't my idea of fun!
You're pushed to the cloakroom, the bell rings again,
So along you plod, back to your den.
'Is everyone here now?' Miss said in a rush,
'Line up nicely now, don't make a fuss.'
'Oh dear,' she said, almost in mime,
'Oh dear, oh dear, *now* look at the time,
Come on now, children, it's 10.02,
Mr Walker won't be very pleased with you.'
Assembly time, all in a row,
'Come on children, not so slow.'
'Mr Walker, *the headmaster,*
Went on for hours, can't he go faster?
After assembly we played some games,
We played ring-a-roses and learnt each other's names.
We had lots of fun until the lunch bell went,
Our mums came to get us, our day was well spent.

Phebe Dwyer (11)
Invicta Grammar School for Girls, Maidstone

I Remember

I remember when the Twin Towers got hit and blown up
How everybody cried and sighed
I remember when David Beckham got red-carded
At the Argentina game
Oh what catastrophe to the crowd!
I remember when the Spice Girls were in fashion
With Ginger Spice's hair, ha, ha!
I remember when the Simpsons first came out
They couldn't even speak to the right tone of the voice
But most of all I remember now -
No Spice Girls
No more major attacks in America
And the Simpsons can speak in time with their voices.

Jordana Parker (14)
King Ethelbert School, Birchington

My Spell

I want to be able to play basketball
But at the moment I play like a fool.
Magical shorts and trainers will look the part
So I will look cool from the very start.
A short sleeve top with a logo on the front
Will make me do a mystical stunt.
Throwing the ball at the basketball hoop
Makes the crowd cheer and whoop.
I shake from side to side on the net
Winning the trophy is a sure bet.
The crowd in the stadium stand and cheer
While I go back to my locker for a cold beer.

Marc Sayer (11)
King Ethelbert School, Birchington

My Spell

Round, round the cauldron go,
I follow very slow!

In I throw a fan's blood,
and a bit of mud!

I pull into the pit stop,
the engine goes pop,
and off I go again!

Round, round the cauldron go,
I follow very slow!

In goes an engine from a car,
and lots of tar!

In go some oiled parts,
it's like lots of carts,
and then I realise I've come first!

Thomas Jordan (11)
King Ethelbert School, Birchington

My Spell

Rat's tail and cat's claw
Bat's tongue, and dog's paws
Frog's leg and human nail
Monkey's cheek and boat's sail
Bird's beak and baby's cry
Animals' lives and duck's wing
Robin's song and hedgehog's spike.

Grant Rutter
King Ethelbert School, Birchington

A Professional Footballer Spell

Ball to foot, foot to goal
Ball to foot, foot to goal,
Round and round the football bubbles
Into the flames, double, double.
Throw the badge gently in the flames
Make me play hundreds of games
In goes the grass, in goes the net
Nearly forgot, fur of my pet
Ball to foot, foot to goal
Ball to foot, foot to goal,
Toss in the head, toss in the kit
So I will have a perfect hit
Run cheetah as fast as you can
Now get yourself into that pan
Last but not least - boots and pads
Now I will be one of the lads.

Luke Spinks (11)
King Ethelbert School, Birchington

Witch's Spell

One stage prop and an actor's tongue
A piece of wooden stage and some Shakespeare plays
Bubble, crackle, spit and swirl
Drink the potion when it's done
A pair of lips to say my lines
Some velvet curtains and an actress' ear
Bubble, crackle, spit and swirl
Drink the potion when it's done
Now drink the potion because it's done
Wait a few seconds now it should have begun.

Bubble, crackle, spit and swirl
Drink the potion when it's done.

John Dean (11)
King Ethelbert School, Birchington

Food Spell

Lizard's gut and toads with frogs,
Dogs' heart and wooden logs,
Worms and bees but also lizards,
Cats we need but mostly a wizard.

Rumble, tumble, apple crumble,
Giggle, wiggle do a squiggle.

Snails and slugs but mostly snakes,
What we need is a big fat cake,
Things live in a sewer just like rats,
There are lots of animals but I like cats.

Rumble, tumble, apple crumble,
Giggle, wiggle do a squiggle.

Liver from a pig,
An old witch's wig,
With a hair of a dog
And a leg of a frog.

Rumble, tumble, apple crumble,
Giggle, wiggle do a squiggle.

With a feather of a duck
And a bit of good luck,
With eye on a fish,
My dinner's on the dish.

Rumble, tumble, apple crumble,
Giggle, wiggle do a squiggle.

Shauni White (11)
King Ethelbert School, Birchington

Rainbow

Rainbow you're as high as a fluffy cloud,
You're as pretty like a butterfly,
You're the best thing I've ever seen,
Please stay and make my dream!

You're as pink as a pink rose,
You're as purple as a sun,
You're as blue as the sky,
You're the best, you're the best,
You're the best thing I've seen!

Please stay you pretty thing,
Why don't you just come in?
You're as multicoloured like a parrot,
You're as cold as a block of ice,
You're so the best thing I've seen!

Paige White (11)
King Ethelbert School, Birchington

My Spell For Thunder And Lightning

Round and round the cauldron go,
Throw in some wind and snow.

Next put in a lizard's tail, rain and hail,
Throw in snow, wind and a snail
And maybe some frog entrails!

Round and round the cauldron go,
Throw in the things below.

Now put in rain and leaves to
Make very loud noises.

Lucy Amos (11)
King Ethelbert School, Birchington

Monster

Cats as a pet,
We're going to get,
In the cauldron goes,
Eagle's nose,
Dragon's tail,
Bats' wing
Bubble, bubble it goes.

Splish,
Splash the cauldron goes,
Bubble pops
Potion flows,
Bubble, bubbles appear.

In goes worms' guts
Rhinos' butt's,
Head of bird,
Lemon curd,
Bubble, bubble it goes.

Splish,
Splash the cauldron goes,
Bubbles pop,
Potion flows,
Bubbles appear.

In goes,
Humans' foot,
Tongue of fox,
Dolphins' mouth,
Cheetahs' legs
And moles' hair,
Bubble, bubble it goes.

Splish,
Splosh the cauldron goes,
Bubbles pop,
Potion flows,
Bubbles, bubbles appear.

Dean Parsons (11)
King Ethelbert School, Birchington

My Spell

In goes a piece of my hair,
Take it under, make my room bare.

In goes the lovely Coke,
Cauldron goes choke, choke, choke.

In goes the cash machine to fill my room,
Lovely money, bloom, bloom, bloom.

In goes the 20 pound note,
Cauldron, bubbles, hubbles and hubbles.

Money, money, just for me,
Fill my room up just for me.

In goes my pussy cat,
Cauldron burn the furry brat.

In goes the piece of paper,
Fill my room up later, later,

Money, money just for me,
Fill my room up just for me.

Sam Clarke (11)
King Ethelbert School, Birchington

Acrostic Poem

J umping on the bouncy castle,
A fter we eat our lunch,
S o then we go on the swings,
M ighty good at swinging,
I n the park,
N ight falls quickly.

G reat fun on the skateboard,
R ight now she is on holiday,
E xtremely good kisser when out of sight,
E xtremely good looks for her mum
N ow I am moving and I say my goodbyes.

Lewis Ward Peakall (11)
King Ethelbert School, Birchington

Mouse Trap

I live in a house
With a mouse
He was brown and fat
He wore a little red hat.

In the morning
He started yawning
As soon as he smelt
He started to yelp.

Cos then he saw a person or more
And ran back into his hut
And stayed there until . . .

He got hungry and went out
And sniffed the air,
He took a few steps and
Snap!

Kayleigh Chapman (13)
King Ethelbert School, Birchington

The Colours Of The Rainbow

Red as roses in a great big field,
Green as grass in my back garden,
Oranges as orange in my fruit bowl,
Blue as the poster I see in the street,
Pink as a pig on my farm,
Yellow as the sun up in the sky,
Black as night when the stars come out,
Mauve as a motor, can I drive around?
White as a cloud that floats in the sky,
Brown as a burger that I put in my mouth.

Adam Pacey (11)
King Ethelbert School, Birchington

The Big Coloured Catz

Jaguar, terror and frightening,
Tail and wispy,
Sliding through the lonely night,
There's his prey and it's gone,
Along the jungle floor.

Tiger arched and huge
Paw as big as a man's head,
He slashes his victim to death
Jealously has had its eye
For fur stripes and all
But it's gone,
Leaving prints on the ground.

Lion as hungry as this predator,
No one will see the difference,
Devours his prey,
Then the king leaves.

Panther as dark as night,
Eye full of lightning,
It gives you a fright,
Watching eyes everywhere.
They follow me
While I'm in his territory.

Leopard as sly as a fox,
Slash and glowing eyes,
Camouflage may see
In the trees out of sight from me.

Cheetah, cheetah,
Fast and quick,
Here and there
Watch your back
He'll be there.

Puma so delicate and light,
Devours prey out of sight,
Then gone in the dead of night,
Come and see my world of beasts
Come in, have a feast.

Lannah Marshall (11)
King Ethelbert School, Birchington

I Remember Poem

I remember . . .
I remember the 9/11
I felt very sad,
I remember the F A Cup Final,
Then I felt proud.

I remember the Spice Girls,
Their posters on my wall,
I remember Boyzone,
Cor! They were so cool.

I remember Playdays,
Singing all day long,
I remember the big 'Pink Panther'
All cuddly and sweet.

I remember big long socks,
With lots of little holes,
I remember Polly Pocket,
They were small as small can go.

I remember, I remember, yes I do remember.

Clair Booker (15)
King Ethelbert School, Birchington

A Poem About My Friend Sophie Bartlett

S he is my best friend
O ften she lets me stay
P erfect she is
H appy all the time, never hardly sad
I mmaculate her room is
E xcited as we meet.

B ut she is very sensitive
A nd she gets hurt easily
R ough she can be
T ime and time again
L ate as she always is
E ven so every day, she comes in with a smile on her face.
T offee pavlora she loves to eat
T akes it to bed, what a treat.

Sarah Mitchell (13)
King Ethelbert School, Birchington

Animals

Animals can run like the wind
Go as slow as a slug
Jump miles
Change colours like the blue sea
Fly as fast as the wind.

Swim like lightning,
Climb trees like bullets
Cheetahs are the fastest in the world
Die just as fast
And start their lives all over again.

Thomas Gibson (11)
King Ethelbert School, Birchington

Thinking Of A Poem

I'm sitting in my English class
Thinking of a poem,
I don't know whether it's going to be hot,
Cold or even snowing.

My friends are whispering quietly,
My mum's probably drinking tea
And as for me?
I'm sitting here thinking of a poem.

I wonder what I'll look like if I dye my hair,
Oh no my mind is wondering,
Someone help me out of here before
I start to scream,
'Come on Gemma it's time for school.'

Oh thank God for that
It was just a scary dream.

Gemma Lee (13)
King Ethelbert School, Birchington

Clouds

I see this thing pass by as slow as a turtle,
It drifts like a bird
And as I watch it go,
The second and the third.

But soon turns grey,
Because it's the end of the day,
I say goodnight,
Although it's really high,
Now it's black as black can be,
I love my clouds.

Tyrrell Martin (12)
King Ethelbert School, Birchington

I Remember

I remember when I was small,
I loved playing catch with my ball.

I remember when I was seven,
I went to a toy shop that looked like Heaven.

I remember Postman Pat,
He ran over his black and white cat.

I remember getting my new stepdad,
I was happy and very glad.

I remember a school trip to France
And my friend who loved to dance.

I remember, I remember.

Sian Fields (14)
King Ethelbert School, Birchington

I Remember

I remember the World Cup,
Lots of people in the pub,
I remember Sarah Payne,
She should have her time again.
I remember Postman Pat,
He was always with his black and white cat.
I remember September the 11th,
People dying a painful death,
I remember the Spice Girls,
People singing their songs to themselves.

Sarah Barar (14)
King Ethelbert School, Birchington

Hannah My Friend

As sweet as sugar
As white as a cloud
As good as a gorilla
As brainy as a brainstorm
As energetic as an elephant.

As cool as an ice cream
As red as a rose
As pink as paper
As careful as a caring mother
As pretty as a panda.

And that is my friend called Hannah.

Natasha Jordan (11)
King Ethelbert School, Birchington

All About Me

S hopping is my hobby,
H andwriting is what I do at school,
A tlases I don't need,
U mbrellas are no match for me,
N ice and neat is what I am,
I enjoy the beach and the lovely sand.

Shauni White (11)
King Ethelbert School, Birchington

Summer

S hining brightly,
U p in the sky,
M ore people at the ice cream van,
M ake our day, keep on shining,
E ven brighter every day,
R ise and shine!

Paige White (11)
King Ethelbert School, Birchington

I Remember

I remember . . .
When Princess Diana died
Everyone was shocked!

I remember . . .
Candle in the Wind, a sort of musical
Memorial for the death of Diana.

I remember . . .
Rosie and Jim on the boat Ragdoll.

I remember . . .
Playing with Action Man,
I used to make him save the world.

I remember . . .
Baseball caps, everyone had one.

I remember . . .
When you used to have water pistol
Fights in the hot, summer sun.

Christopher Nicholls (14)
King Ethelbert School, Birchington

Puppy And Hippo

As beautiful as a rose,
Elegant as a rhinoceros,
Slower than the wind,
It can go,
My favourite hippo.

As sweet as sugar,
So fluffy as a rug,
Sleeping like a baby,
In his kennel,
After his food, my puppy.

Naomi Davis (12)
King Ethelbert School, Birchington

I Remember Poem

I remember when my grandad died,
I remember when Steps first came out,
I loved them so much,
I remember when Hollyoaks first came out,
It was brilliant,
I remember when everyone was wearing dungarees, yuck, yuck,
I remember Barbie and her long blonde hair,
I remember when I saw Atomic Kitten,
I was screaming all night,
I remember when I was in infant school
And we played all the time.
I remember when we first met my stepdad
I was really glad my mum was happy,
I remember the day I got my first bike, with no stabilisers,
I remember the day my little sister was born
She was like my princess.

Kayleigh Morris (14)
King Ethelbert School, Birchington

I Remember

I remember my first bun,
I remember going to the carnival, it was fun,
I remember the Beatles, they're now dead,
I remember Bill and Ben, the flowerpot men,
I remember people with fluffy hair,
I remember my toy bear with curly hair,
I remember Postman Pat with his black and white cat,
I remember playing with a Hallowe'en bat.

Jay Dawson (14)
King Ethelbert School, Birchington

I Remember

I remember
I remember when Princess Diana died in a crash,
England was in pieces.

I remember
I remember the Spice Girls, Girl Power.

I remember
I remember Peter Pan the video,
Oh if only
I could go to Neverland.

I remember
I remember wearing bright colours,
Hot pants and boob tubes,
We looked like rainbows.

But most of all I remember,
I remember Hugnug my dinosaur,
I used to suck my thumb and he used to comfort me.

Amy Johncock (14)
King Ethelbert School, Birchington

My Acrostic Poem

T otal mess this acrostic poem
H elp me, save me
O r I will die in this classroom
M arvellous I have 30 minutes left
A dictionary should help me
S o there are no books left, oh great.

H ow am I going to do it now?
O h Sir is not going to like this,
W hy is it happening to me?
E nglish was never my best subject.

Thomas Howe (11)
King Ethelbert School, Birchington

I Remember

I remember the horror of 9/11
I remember when England done so
Well in the World Cup.

I remember when I had a BB gun,
I remember Eminem's first song.

I remember Jarule,
I remember when I watched Top Cat.

I remember when Batman was good,
I remember when I wanted TN's.

I remember my remote control car,
I remember, I remember, I remember.

Christian Blow (14)
King Ethelbert School, Birchington

I Can't Smile Without You

This poem is like the song
Even though it needs a bit of a ding-dong,
I need you there,
To help me through,
Because I just can't smile without you,
I need some help,
To make me better,
Also a boyfriend,
To write a love letter,
I need you there,
To help me through,
Because I just can't smile without you.

Hayley Morgan (13)
King Ethelbert School, Birchington

I Remember

I remember when I was young,
I wore frilly hats in the summer's sun.

I remember when I was three,
I used to watch Barney.

I remember the Twin Towers,
The people that died and all the flowers.

I remember Gareth Gates,
I told my cousins we were mates.

I remember Postman Pat,
He ran over his black and white cat.

I remember when I was small,
I used to throw my basketball.

I remember my trip to France,
I was so excited I started to dance.

Natalie Gordon (14)
King Ethelbert School, Birchington

Holidays

Sun, sea and sand are the beauties of a holiday,
Go for a week but you wish for home to stay away,
Home is light years away when you are on the beach,
Wet sand clings to you like you are a leech,
Holidays are a time to be very happy,
But when you return you are not a happy chappy,
Sunburn and school is still to come,
And when you get home you miss the fun,
But relax and enjoy being at home,
Because in the end, it's better than Spain or Rome.

Joanne Nolan (13)
King Ethelbert School, Birchington

Finally Asleep

I got into bed and
Tucked myself in,
I decided to read instead,
Then I thought, *I haven't*
Brushed my teeth,
Brush, brush, brush.
I got into bed and
Tucked myself in,
Then I remembered I
Hadn't said goodnight
To Mum and Dad.
Kiss, goodnight, kiss, goodnight,
I got into bed and
Tucked myself in.
Then I thought, *my homework,*
It's due in tomorrow,
Write, scribble, write, scribble.
I got into bed and tucked
Myself in, then I thought, *the*
Hamster needs feeding,
Crunch, crunch, crunch,
I got into bed and
Tucked myself in,
And went to sleep.
Snore, snore, snore,
I woke up to
Ring, ring, ring,
My alarm clock
That stupid thing!

Kelly Wills (13)
King Ethelbert School, Birchington

I Remember

I remember the Iraq war,
When people were dying for their country.

September 11th was a touching day,
When many people had nothing to say.
Nothing but anger,
The world's a different place,
Many people shamed the human race.
Why are we here?
Is it to cause pain?
There is emptiness in some of the human race.

But now that is over and done with,
I remember back, way long ago, Will Smith was in the top ten
And many girls thought so, I would sit in my room playing out loud
Summertime album with only my sister Jolene around.

I remember the 80s when kids would only wear baggy clothes
They would walk around
With their trousers down by their toes.

I remember when I was young, Eastenders
Would be the word that everyone would know about
They would come to school with nothing else to talk about.

I remember when I was a little girl,
Barbie was the toy,
That every girl would dream about.

Now it has changed
I'm all grown up
There are no baggy trousers
And no toy to talk about.

Jayne Boon (15)
King Ethelbert School, Birchington

I Remember Poem

I remember . . .
The excitement of the new millennium.

I remember . . .
The terrible death of Princess Diana.

I remember . . .
Singing along to the Spice Girls.

I remember . . .
Postman Pat, everyone watched it on television.

I remember . . .
Posters of Boyzone hanging on my wall.

I remember . . .
Playing with my Barbies.

I remember . . .
Wearing my wonderful, new frilly dress.

I remember . . .
Wearing my first new pair of Barbie trainers.

I remember . . .
My stripy long socks.

I remember . . .
My favourite video 'Beauty and the Beast.'

I remember . . .
When the Twin Towers fell to the ground.

I remember it all.

Lisa Wilkinson (15)
King Ethelbert School, Birchington

I Remember

I remember the happy days when England won the World Cup,
Even though I was not alive then,
I've seen it so many times I feel like I was there.

I remember when I used to watch Rosy and Jim,
I used to get so excited when it started.

I remember 9/11,
When I heard about the Two Towers,
I was really sad and shocked.

I remember when Princess Diana died,
I felt heart broken.

I remember Elton John doing a song about the death of Diana,
My mum nearly cried and my heart sank,
It was called 'Candle in the Wind'.

I remember when I used to play with Action Men,
I used to have so much fun,
It was the best thing in the world to me.

Scott Moreton (14)
King Ethelbert School, Birchington

Chicken Head

Round about the chicken goes,
Up and down the chicken blow,
Singing a song while it sleeps,
Having a drink while it leaps,
As the chicken is going in,
Forget the head, it's going in the bin,
Put his legs in the tin,
It's not dead, stab it with a pin.

Billy Hewitt (11)
King Ethelbert School, Birchington

Childhood

Childhood is like a present,
Wrapped tightly with a bow,
Causing worry and excitement,
Fear and enlightenment,
Let the beauty of childhood unfold.

Childhood is like a computer,
It evolves as life moves on.
It gets updated,
Marked and rated,
But children will move on.

Childhood is like music script,
With markings scribbled on.
It ticks and it tocks,
And then rings as it stops,
As children have moved on.

Childhood is like a candle,
It glows then it's gone.
It grows and it grows,
And then becomes low,
As children have moved on.

Childhood is precious,
A time for fun and rhymes.
For innocence and lying,
Laughing and crying,
Keep memories of these precious times.

Elizabeth Goudsmit (12)
Lady Eleanor Howes, Hampton

Oliver's Marvellous Medicine

Into my pot I will put . . .
Wing of dinosaur and spider's foot,
Head of a Simon, teeth of a cat,
Blood of a vampire and squeak of a rat.
A brain from a beetle,
A tail from a mouse.
Mix it together
With monsters' bloody eyes,
Use it for sucking people's minds.

Oliver Murray-Brown (12)
Marjorie McClure School, Chislehurst

I Like

I like music,
I have got lots of friends,
Sometimes I go out for days with my family,
I like swimming, I go every day,
Exciting, warm, happy.
Winning at bowling I like.
I won a medal.

Amy Thompson (16)
Marjorie McClure School, Chislehurst

Fairy-Tale Princess

I like my new school,
I am going to be
The fairy princess, Josie.
Handsome Jack will be my prince
And he will kill the dragon.
Really cool.

Josie Keeler (12)
Marjorie McClure School, Chislehurst

Gunners At Highbury

G reatest
U sually
N ever
N asty
E ntertaining
R arely
S ent off.

A rsenal
T op team.

H ighest
I wish I was there
G oal
H enry to
B ergkamp
U p the Arsenal
R oar
Y es!

Thomas Clements (14)
Marjorie McClure School, Chislehurst

The Magic Princess

Princess Olivia was walking down the street
When she saw the evil witch she had to meet.
Then the witch made a spell and turned her into a dove.
All that can break the spell is true love.
Then the witch locked the princess in a well
Under a spell.
The princess shouted, *'Help!'*
All that she hears is a dog yelp.
The prince saves the princess, fights the witch
And finishes her off by pushing her in a ditch
And they live happily ever after.

Kimberley O'Connor (12)
Marjorie McClure School, Chislehurst

Music

In my bedroom
Sitting on my chair

I put on my earphones
To listen to Sugarbabes.

Racks of CDs,
I can't fit any more in.

I play them 24/7
Turn up the volume,

Hear the sounds,
Listen to voices.

I am happy,
Let's dance.

Nicki Harper (14)
Marjorie McClure School, Chislehurst

The London Eye

I liked being up in the air, looking at all the buildings,
I liked looking at all of London,
I enjoyed the flight so much,
I saw Big Ben, the big building which had a clock on it and bells inside.
The Houses of Parliament looked clean and old.
I saw the River Thames, it looked very dirty.
I saw Waterloo Bridge.
I saw cars on the bridge, going by.

Christian Bush (13)
Marjorie McClure School, Chislehurst

Football Match

I wish I could go to a football match
Dad, please take me
Will it be noisy?
Rubbish on pitch
Lots of cheering fans
It's a goal!
Oranges at half-time
Crowds standing shouting
Come on, come on
Penalty
Players fighting, punch-up
Referee blows his whistle
I wish I could go to a football match.

Paul Poulton (14)
Marjorie McClure School, Chislehurst

The Ocean

I'm sailing in a small boat on the ocean,
All I can see is the sky and the sea,
Under the water it is very busy,
If I could look under the water I would see
Millions of brightly coloured fish flashing.
On the seabed is a shipwrecked pirate ship,
It is brown and red with rust,
Everything on it has bust,
The sand on the bottom looks like dust,
(People on beaches leave their rubbish behind.)
The seabed is like the Earth's crust,
It's such a shame, I think they should mind.

Ethan Middleton (13)
Marjorie McClure School, Chislehurst

Snooker

S hoot the balls in the pocket,
N ever try to cheat,
O ver the colour balls,
O ver the red balls,
K eep your cue in shape,
E nd the game in style.
R ealise that you have won.

C halk up your cue,
H andshake with your opponent,
A dd a point after you pot,
M ake it an easy game,
P ot all the balls left on the table
I 'm thinking how I am going to play my next shot,
O h darn, next time lucky,
N othing will stop me in snooker,
S uddenly I pot the black,
H olding my cue with patience,
I nform the ref he is cheating,
P at the table to say, *'Well done,* better luck next time.'

Vimal Patel (13)
Marjorie McClure School, Chislehurst

When I Look Out Of My Window

When I look out of my window in the morning I see
Grey mist floating through the air.

When I look out of my window I see
Raindrops dripping off the washing line cover.

When I look out of my window I see
Trees blowing this way and that.

When I look out of my window I see
The sky is still dark.

Marie Murray (11)
Marjorie McClure School, Chislehurst

Horses

My pretend horse called Prince can kick but is friendly.
I play horses with Katie, my best friend, every day at break time
And lunchtime.
At my stables I ride my *favourite* pony, Jimmy,
He can be naughty.
My *favourite* leader is Alice, she gives me Sheltie books.
She says she's going to give me some Animal Ark books.
She always leads me.
There are more ponies, there's Promise, Blue, Comet, Lucky, Tilly,
Stompey, Twiggy, Pickles, Charley and Mischief.

Harriet Steddy (11)
Marjorie McClure School, Chislehurst

Motorbikes!

Motorbikes are faster than rockets plunging in mid-air.

The engine roars louder than a lion,
The rider shakes like an earthquake
The wheels kick the dirt up like a dragster,
It speeds round sharp corners
Like bolts of lightning,
The metalwork glistens in the sun.
The paintwork is smooth and
Shiny.
The slope is big and strong and smooths the bumps.
I did a jump, a bunny hop and a
Wheelie and finished on my front
Wheel.

Christopher Cook (11)
Rowhill School, Dartford

Tigers

Tigers, tigers are scary,
Tigers, tigers are fast,
Tigers, tigers make a big roar,
Tigers are my favourite animal
Because they are very furry,
Sometimes they look at me and roar through the grass,
Then they go back to sleep
Up in the nice, comfy bed
Way up on the hill.

Victoria Maione (13)
Rowhill School, Dartford

A Tree

There is a tree lying down
Like a giant with torn out roots
Instead of feet
It is like a ship sailing far out to sea.
It has places to hide and climb and swing on.
It will never stand up
Not ever!

Zoe Maynard (12)
Rowhill School, Dartford

Dolphins

Dolphins are always pleased to meet you,
Their skin is beautiful, blue or grey,
They jump up and down in the sea,
They are always pleased to see me,
They do tricks to amaze you.

Danielle Caddick (12)
Rowhill School, Dartford

So Distant!

The tide is out, I cannot swim.
I have my trunks,
I have my towel,
I have my goggles
All ready, but I cannot swim.

I listen to the sea,
I listen to the wind,
I listen to the screech of the gulls,
All ready, but I cannot swim.

I eat my sandwiches,
I drink my lemonade,
I crunch my crisps,
All ready, but I cannot swim.

Frustration mounting,
Heart beating,
Mind racing,
All ready, but I still cannot swim.

A friend arrives,
We talk
And look out to sea,
All ready, and now the sea approaches.

The sky brightens,
My hopes rise,
My body tenses,
All ready, the sea washes over my feet,

I flow through the water with mighty strokes,
I crawl back to the shore exhausted,
My homework is done!

Edward Price (14)
Ryde School, Isle Of Wight

Drowning

Held underwater by an invisible hand,
Trying to reach the surface, everyone else can,
Bubbles escape,
Lungs scream,
The hand won't relent.

Calm and dodge, but the hand still holds,
Pushing you down further, grows even more bold,
Sight blurs,
Ears pop,
The hand won't relent.

Desperate and searching, but the hand knows your every move,
Swerving and swirling, moving with you,
Lungs fill,
Head aches,
The hand won't relent.

Angry now bitten, the hand grasps,
Squeezing the life out, bubbles go up with a gasp,
Dying slowly,
Brain waterlogged,
The hand now relents.

Kicking and paddling the surface is broken,
Gulping and gasping for air.
You look around you and see no one,
The hand was never there.

Rosanna Hounslow (14)
Ryde School, Isle Of Wight

Hidden Talent

Oh! how I'd love to be an artist
Standing back so superior and vain,
My work displayed in corridors,
On walls and windowpanes.
But just in case you didn't know,
I've heard it all before,
'Your work's as desirable as paw prints on the floor.'

Now . . .

These hands do hold a forte
Of which you may not be aware,
They caress a size five rugby ball
As I dodge up the pitch with flair.
My hands may not be aesthetic,
They can neither sculpt nor paint,
But watch me on the rugby pitch and I bet I make you faint!

Matthew Foster (13)
Ryde School, Isle Of Wight

Hidden Talent

In the tool shed,
he looks at the tools in bewilderment,
like a blind man trying to imagine colour.
He looks at the tools in wonder,
knowing there must be a purpose for each tool.

At the microphone,
he steps forward, starts to sing;
the microphone screeches like a lamb to the abattoir.
He does not know the sounds coming
like a waterfall from this mouth,
is this destiny or idiocy?

On the football pitch,
he weaves the ball in and out of the opponents,
like a thread in an electric sewing machine,
and swings the cross in.

Liam O'Flynn (13)
Ryde School, Isle Of Wight

Honour

The shouts of men
As limbs fly foul;
They seem to think in honour.
Is it honour to die
In mud-ridden lands alone?

The words, 'Over the top,'
As men topple and die.
Is this honour?

The rain, the suffering
Is spoken in all but word.

The rain beats on,
Blisters burn,
Blasts and gunfire are near.
The fire rages and burns within.

I am nothing anymore.

Sam Scadgell (15)
Ryde School, Isle Of Wight

The Hidden Talent

Running
Huffing and puffing like a steam engine,
dirt flicking up at her calves.
The wind blows against her poor, jelly-like legs.

Swimming
Water pushing against her every move,
the water streaming into her stinging red eyes.
Her arms weakened by lack of energy.

History
Dates and times shooting at her from ever direction,
like World War II, she stares at the window, blank minded.
She sits there in hunger of the bell.

Violin
She stands and plays the melody to the listening world,
with joy on every note, her heart laden with delight.
Talent pouring over the stage. The applause shakes the Earth.

Xenita Taylor (13)
Ryde School, Isle Of Wight

I Am A Little Piggy

There is a pig inside me
He's tubby, short and stout,
He really makes me angry
But he just won't come out.

He squeaks and squeals out loud
Which really makes him proud,
Snorting and squeaking
When I start speaking,
It really gets me down.

This pig is never full,
He always wants a snack,
I ask my mum for food,
She offers me a smack.

I now know how to feed him,
I give him a Brussels sprout,
He doesn't really like it,
I think he's just come out.

Hannah Downton (12)
St Mary's Middle School, Dorchester

Stormy Ocean

The sea is very rough and the waves go up
                                    and
                                        down,
Boats are upside down and tnorf-ot-kcab.

The boats look like floating Toblerone bars,
They are upon the fizz of blue lemonade,
The wind is a sneeze from the heavens,
The waves are the reading from a heart monitor.
The clouds are wire wool,
Yet this verse is flat and calm.

Oliver Denton (11)
Solent Middle School, Cowes

The Writer Of This Poem

(A poem in the style of Roger McGough)

The writer of this poem . . .
Is as sleek as a shark,
As thick as a tree,
As tall as an ark.

As sharp as a bread knife,
As solid as a rock,
As bold as a boulder,
As strong as a block.

As fast as a jet plane,
As clever as a book,
As skilled as a blacksmith,
As tricky as a crook.

The writer of this poem
Is a very clever chap,
He's one in a million,
So give him a clap.

James Tomkins (12)
Solent Middle School, Cowes

Spider

Spider, spider, let me be
As quiet as you and I can be.
I fly around on a spider's web,
It is just like hanging from a thread.

Melanie Rock (11)
Solent Middle School, Cowes

Bang!

Bang! 'Owwww!'
'Stop it,' shouted Dad.
Bang!
Bang!
'Owwww!'
'Stop it or I will take it off you.'
'No you won't.'
Bang!
'I warned you,'
Snatch.
'Ha, ha.'
Dad took it off me.
Bang!
'Stop, you lied to me.'
I snatched it back and ran.
I hope he doesn't take it off me again.

Sam Tyson (11)
Solent Middle School, Cowes

How Can I Not Remember It?

Playing around, shoot, *smash,*
Shatter, silence.
Anger, anger, everywhere,
My mum shouting,
I am in big trouble,
Gun so powerful, shocking fright,
So fast it went,
It shocked my eyes,
Trying to get away with it,
I don't know if I will,
Will I escape from being grounded?

Zoe Minshull (11)
Solent Middle School, Cowes

The Writer Of This Poem

(A poem in the style of Roger McGough)

The writer of this poem . . .
Is positively the worst
At writing rhyming poetry,
Although this is his first.

As cunning as a fox,
As annoying as a bee,
As cool as a cucumber,
As jumpy as a flea.

As fierce as a bull,
As quick as a cheetah,
As patient as a spider,
Smarter than your teacher.

So this is the end,
It is starting to unfold,
Please 'scuse this silly rhyme,
As he's only 12 years old.

Adam Mitchell (12)
Solent Middle School, Cowes

The Writer Of This Poem

(In the style of Roger McGough)

The writer of this poem . . .
Is as quick as a flea,
As strong as a bear
And as smart as can be.

As good as Jamie Oliver,
As tasty as a meal,
As sharp as a sword and
As sturdy as a shield.

As tough as a hitman.
As hard as nails,
As stealthy as a shadow,
As balanced as scales.

The writer of this poem
Is totally amazing
And if you believe that,
You'll believe anything!

Josh Pointing (12)
Solent Middle School, Cowes

The Writer Of This Poem

(In the style of Roger McGough)

The writer of this poem . . .
Is quietly laid back,
As quick as a snail,
As blind as a bat.

As strong as a twig,
As thick as a post,
As bold as a mouse,
As awake as a sloth.

As rich as a peasant,
As noisy as a thud,
As elegant as a hippo,
As clean as mud.

The writer of this poem
Isn't that glamorous as you can see,
But all of my friends like me
Just being me!

Helen Baggett (12)
Solent Middle School, Cowes

The Writer Of This Poem

(In the style of Roger McGough)

The writer of this poem . . .
Is cooler than a fridge,
As quick as a Ferrari,
As sturdy as a bridge.

As sharp as a knife,
As cunning as a fox,
As tall as a skyscraper,
As useful as a box.

As clever as a scientist,
As deep as a lake,
As brave as a Roman,
As smooth as a milkshake.

The writer of this poem
Is amazingly great,
He's the best poet ever,
(Or so says his mate.)

Ben Green (12)
Solent Middle School, Cowes

The Writer Of This Poem

(In the style of Roger McGough)

The writer of this poem . . .
Is as tall as a tree,
As ginger as a fire,
As skinny as can be.

As wild as the wind,
As bright as a star,
As weird as a wallaby,
As clean as a car.

As fast as a whip,
As sticky as glue,
As smart as Saturn,
As scary as a *boo!*

The writer of this poem
Is as crazy as a cow,
She could not write these poems
And is still no better now!

Rachel Bennett (12)
Solent Middle School, Cowes

When I Was Playing Cricket

Smack!
I hit the ball sky high,
Bang!
It hit my brother on the head,
Thud!
He hit the ground,
He was out - cold.
My mum bellowed from inside,
'Call an ambulance.'
The ambulance arrived,
We got in and we were on the way to the hospital,
Josh woke up.
We were there for about an hour,
Then we went.
Slam!
Mum slammed the door and sent me up to my room without any tea,
While my brother was downstairs eating his KFC and watching TV.

Joe Moody (11)
Solent Middle School, Cowes

Mistakes

Everyone is a suspect when it comes to mistakes,
So why can't people forget the ones I have made?
I often try to be someone else, just to fit in,
I try to be myself, but I just can't win.
If they don't like me for me, I can't call them friends,
So why do I still try to change, just to please them?

I hate myself for what I have done,
But I made mistakes. Why can't they move on?

I distanced myself from those who are true friends,
I tried to change for others, so I forgot about them,
I wish I could turn back time, but it can't be done.
I can only say sorry for me ever hurting anyone.

I wonder why there is one friend who has stuck by me,
No one else has, so why has she?
I try to forget everything and put it behind me,
But everywhere I go, people tell, so others think differently.
I try to make new friends but my mistakes are heard,
So now they judge me, before I ever say a word.

I hate myself and I always will,
But I made mistakes.

Everyone has.

Everyone will.

Marie Willoughby (16)
Sunbury Manor School, Sunbury-on-Thames

Brussels

People get frustrated on them,
Cars overheat on them,
Motorways
I hate that stuff.

Cut you up doing it,
Mainly old people doing it,
Mad driving,
I hate that stuff.

Have to get up early for it,
Work so much at it,
School,
I hate that stuff.

You fight with them,
You argue with them,
Brothers and sisters,
I hate that stuff.

Kids hate them,
Eat roast dinner with them,
Brussels,
I hate that stuff.

Freddy Colaluca (13)
The Cedars School, Maidstone

My Friend

M y friend Rory
Y ells sometimes.

F un to be with,
R ory plays on his PlayStation 2
I think he's funny,
E nds up doing wrestling on me,
N ever goes anywhere else,
D rinks Diet Coke a lot.

Lloyd Hatcher (12)
The Cedars School, Maidstone

My Dad John

M y dad is a mechanic and most of the time he
Y ells at me for being bad.

D ad is okay to talk to if he is in a good mood
A nd he can be a good listener.
D ark hair, fattish, big built and tall.

J okes around sometimes,
O n cars working all the time.
H elps me fix all different things
N ever up for playing football.

Michael Tsouri (14)
The Cedars School, Maidstone

Kenning

A lead puller
A bird chaser
A teddy ripper
A fur scuffer
A rabbit galloper
A door scratcher
A house walker
A meat eater.

I am a . . . ?

Adam Weston (12)
The Cedars School, Maidstone

Kenning

A tree liver
A scary starer

A perfect hider
A night flyer

A loud shrieker
A quiet sleeper

A food scavenger
A silent creeper

An egg layer
A night hunter

I am a . . .

Toni Head (13)
The Cedars School, Maidstone

My Sister

M akes me laugh
Y aps a lot

S he screeches
I nsists on wearing pink
S he's got a sweet smile
T ears when she can't get her own way,
E very day watches videos,
R eally, really spoilt.

Philip Hunt (13)
The Cedars School, Maidstone

The Three Little Pigs
The Funny Version

There once was a mother pig
Who always wore a wig;
But one day she caught it alight.
She leant over the hob
And accidentally hit the knob.
Now she's not a very pretty sight.

Mother pig had four sons,
Who, like her, weighed tons;
But it wasn't very good for them at all.
The farmer chased them for fun.
And he used his gun
When a pig didn't make it to the wall.

The family was sad
And they must have been mad;
As their mum let them all leave home.
On their way out
She kissed each one's snout
And said they must always phone.

The first porky pig
Had a pile of twigs
So he used them to build a lovely house.
He built it rather well,
Though it was very hard to tell;
Whether the house was even fit for a mouse.

The second little piggy
Said he was too biggy
So he bought a big bag of straw.
He built it rather quick
And he was very sick
When he cut his porky leg with a saw.

To the other's great surprise,
The third pig was wise
'Cause he built his little house out of bricks.
He was very proud indeed
And he was in the lead
Of the other piggy with the sticks.

The pigs were very pleased
But not when they were seized
By the wolf that had a terrifying grin.
He got his knife and fork
And the piggies said, 'We're pork!'
But they got away by kicking his shin.

Jodie Newland (12)
Townley Grammar School, Bexleyheath

Soldier

Cover the stone walls with your blood, soldier,
Let tears flow deep into valleys underground,
Time will not heal the wounds on your soul,
Never will the flag of white be waved
As you meet eye to eye
With your despised foe.

Is he any different from you, soldier?
Fuelled by an unjust and meaningless hatred,
Murdering the innocent and spilling his guts,
To please a country he's never really been fond of.

Water will not wash away your crimes, soldier,
Or the scars in your mind.
Long live your country,
At the price of your life.

Parminder Kaur Sahota (15)
Villiers High School, Southall

Ice Queen

The Ice Queen sits on her diamond throne,
In her palace of ice,
Glaring up at the midnight stars
Through her glassy roof.
Her eyes are hard, bitter,
Her stare is like an army of steel arrows,
Bearing down upon the innocent victim.
A long cascade of silvery hair
Flows down her rigid back,
Her voice is a freezing rush
Of gushing water,
Sounding of ringing crystal
And screeching demons.
She wears a dress of finely spun silk,
Blue and silver elegance.
Sharp ceiling icicles pierce the frosty air
Like daggers through a cloud.
Slowly she stands,
Walks gracefully across the room.
With every step becoming angrier,
A burning hatred rages in her heart of fire.
She reaches for a glistening icicle
And with one white hand
Crushes it to powdery snow.
Shattered ice litters the floor.
The shadow of a thick, ghostly cloud
Crosses the palace grounds,
Blocking out the moon's bright light.
Silent ripples cross the icy lake.
On the horizon, a pale pink light appears,
A soft, warm magenta.
Blankets of snow resting on fir branches
Begin to melt away.
Delicate young blossoms
Reach towards the new light.
Pearls of dew shine as a powerful energy
Stretches across the land.

The benign spring sun shines gloriously,
But is the Ice Queen's mortal enemy.
She screams in fury, trembling,
A cracking noise sounds.
The ice palace is falling . . .
Great shards of ice
Tumble off the Ice Queen's looming mountain,
Until all that is left
Is a shimmering ocean of water and icebergs.
Gleaming in the sunshine
And a torn dress of finely spun silk,
Floating helplessly across the surface.

Amy Liebthal (14)
Wilmington Grammar School for Girls, Dartford

Horses

Galloping through the fields
Trotting around the ring
Hooves splashing in the shallows
Manes are flicking up.
Clip-clop,
They race the clock
Splish, splash,
They always crash.
These are the noises I hear.
Some are treated well
And some are treated badly,
Some are good-looking,
Others aren't.
Whatever breed they are,
Whatever they look like,
They'll always have one big fan
And that is *me!*

Emily Allen (12)
Wilmington Grammar School for Girls, Dartford

My Worst Nightmare

I had a terrible nightmare
I woke up in a sweat,
with my heart really racing
and my clothes wringing wet.

I dreamt there was no football,
not one game in the land,
for; in my worst dream of all time,
football had been banned.

The stadiums had been closed
the pitches all dug up,
old ladies now grew flowers
inside the great World Cup.

Footballs had been flattened
and mascots set quite free,
all football players without a job
were sent away to sea.

The whole thing was a disaster;
my worst nightmare of all,
for what would we ever do
in a world without football?

Jessica Hibberd (12)
Wilmington Grammar School for Girls, Dartford

Fireworks

F ire burning all around
I gnited coals glowing
R ed and bright
E verything illuminated
W hirls of colour in the sky
O range, yellow, green and
R ed
K ids playing with
S parklers.

Laura Spitter (13)
Wilmington Grammar School for Girls, Dartford

Reincarnation

To think that this is not the first time I was on this planet
To think that I might have made new friends
With old friends from the past

How I could have a different allergy
Or my eyes are a different colour

We could speak another language
Have different names

We could fulfil dreams which was not done in life previously

We could have been poor but now rich
Sick but now healthy
Hating but now caring
Dangerous but now peaceful

Who knows what we could have been like before?
You will never find out,
Or will you?

Sharona Doyle (13)
Wilmington Grammar School for Girls, Dartford

Old Man

Old man sits and stares,
I wonder if he has any cares.
His clothes in rags,
Watching blowing paper bags.
He's got messy hair,
But he doesn't care.
Where is he from? Nobody knows,
His shoes have holes so I can see his toes.
What is he thinking and why?
As he sees the people passing by.
He spends his life day in and day out,
On his bench with no hassle that we can all live without.
I walk past the bench
And what do I see . . . ?

Laura Dalton (13)
Wilmington Grammar School for Girls, Dartford

Little Hidden People

Tiptoeing home through the forest
You hear a little squeak
It's coming from down below
Coming from your feet.

You look and see
Then think again
Glance and you will see
That you have dropped your key.

Then you hear a dance and tune
Coming from your right
Once turned you see what is meant to be
The forest in your sight.

You know they're there but somehow aren't
The creatures that you hear
These creatures are the *fairies*
Who really are not fair.

Katharine Leach (13)
Wilmington Grammar School for Girls, Dartford

Fly

I wonder what it's like to fly higher than a house
Above the treetops
Above the clouds?

I wonder what it's like to see the sights
Beautiful things
Things you only see on aeroplane flights?

I wonder what it's like to soar above the sky?
The sky would be the limit
If I could fly.

Charlotte Lynch (11)
Wilmington Grammar School for Girls, Dartford

The Red Hills Of India

The red hills of India how they swoop and curve
The red hills of India how they whoop and serve
They serve the sunshine bold and bright
They serve the moon throughout the night
They're nice and quiet like a fox
They're a free spirit trapped in a box

A free spirit what is that,
Is it a thing like a bat?
Is it a dog or a rug?
Is it a free flying bug?
Is it a fly flying high in the sky?
Is it a mum saying, 'My oh my'?

Mums, they're funny things
Can they fly? Do they have wings?

Kim Rackley (12)
Wilmington Grammar School for Girls, Dartford

Sisters Forever

We're not always friends
But our love will never end
We quarrel and fight
All through the night
We'll always be there for each other.

We will argue over silly things
Like how in games she always wins
We sing and we shout
Her love I'll never doubt
We'll always be there for each other.

So when we're feeling low
We know just where to go
We stick up for each other
Love one another
We'll always be there for each other.

Hannah Collcutt (13)
Wilmington Grammar School for Girls, Dartford

Decisions

So many things are in my mind,
Are they harsh and vicious,
Or careful and kind?
I cannot decide,
I cannot choose,
Thoughts and questions are on the loose.
It's time to conclude what I want to do,
Some would sharply decide,
But I haven't a clue.
The bitterness of confusion,
Lay still in my head,
My brain is a puzzle,
My life's not been fed.
All this is so negative,
What must I now do?
Run from imagination?
It's not up to you.
My choice is in hand,
I deal with these questions,
But how must I cope,
With these headaches and tensions?
My future's ahead of me,
The step is progressing,
As now I go on my words are undressing.
Nothing can change now,
I do what I wish.
The problems are solving,
My thought is now this.
To think of things naturally
And picture pure bliss.

Nicola Munns (13)
Wilmington Grammar School for Girls, Dartford

Why?

Dear God
I want to ask you what I don't understand
When you made Earth and you made man
Why did you make us so we could feel pain?
Why do we look to hurt and then look for blame?
Why do we have wars when there's no reason to attack?
Why are we alone when we need a friend to watch our back?
Why do we never think of others and how they might feel?
Why do you let us make weapons and learn to use them to kill?
Why are we selfish? Why are we made so we can cry?
Why do we have to feel upset? Why do you let people die?
Why is plenty never enough? Why are humans obsessed with greed
And why is help never there when you're in need?
Why do we get mad and go over the top?
Why can't you change it? Why can't you make it stop?
Why is life so difficult? Why is life made so tough?
Why does it have to happen?
Haven't we suffered enough?

Marie Telfer (12)
Wilmington Grammar School for Girls, Dartford

What Is A Friend?

A friend is someone you can trust,
They don't leave you standing on your own,
They help you with homework
And are there when you need them.

A real friend will always stay,
A friend is there night and day,
A real friend will take your tears away,
But most of all they won't run away.

Jacqui Phillips (14)
Wilmington Grammar School for Girls, Dartford

A Queen's Delight

On a cold winter's day I sew by the fire
In my gowns I am dressed by maids that never tire.
They choose me a dress and soft velvet shoes
This washes away my winter blues.
I eat from a banquet as my carriage waits still
I wish for the day to be full of goodwill.
The birds in the garden sing of good cheer
But I must eat fast as lateness I fear.
My gowns are brushed down and make-up applied
Hair curled into a bun and gracefully tied.
I step into the carriage of gold that gleams
It's perfect - more than any woman dreams.
The air bites my face as its coldness I feel
This whole experience it must be unreal.
The snow gently falls on roofs of thatch
It's magical - there must be a catch!
Off to the ball! The horses run swift
A feeling inside gives me a lift.
As the carriage arrives I see a great sight
More than one thousand people dancing into the night.
A silence falls around the glistening hall
The queen has arrived at the fairy-tale ball.

Rachel Delman (13)
Wilmington Grammar School for Girls, Dartford

My Sister

S isters, sisters, big and small
I have a sister she's quite tall
S he is a pain believe it or not
T he times were better when she slept in a cot
E ven though she cries all the time
R eally I love her like a gold dime!

Carmen Homewood (11)
Wilmington Grammar School for Girls, Dartford

The Frilly Lizard

The gentle lizard comes out at night,
When he's not sleeping in the sand.
He keeps a careful eye out,
While he's leaping over land.

The lizard dreams of climbing trees,
Way above the ground.
Then gracefully climbing down again.
Without a single sound.

Then suddenly there's a noise,
A noise not far away.
He gently clambers closer
And a coral snake, there he lay.

The lizard stands ready, ready to pounce
And the snake just lies there still.
He thought the snake might move a bit,
But he didn't, so it's in for the kill.

At the last moment the snake comes up
And gives an evil glare,
But the lizard he is ready;
His frill comes up like flares.

The snake does not survive
And the lizard is alive
And gracefully leaps back home again,
Then falls asleep with pride!

Emily Irving (12)
Wilmington Grammar School for Girls, Dartford

Jungle Awakes

As the day dawns, the jungle awakes,
Monkeys throw nuts, teasing a snake.
A koala blearily opens one eye,
Watching a butterfly come fluttering by.
The lemurs jump from tree to tree,
Disturbing the parrots, who screech nervously.
Down by the water hole, giraffes cluster,
Whilst rhinos charge with all the strength they can muster.

Tiger cubs leap and chase their tails,
With lizards watching them, flashing their scales.
Gorillas with young, having rides on Mum's back
And tree frogs, all colours, jump from canopy black.

The girl gave a sigh and laid down her pen
And thought of all the animals we had back then.

Kirsty Mackay (11)
Wilmington Grammar School for Girls, Dartford

Nightlife

The stars above light up the sky,
As though they are from God's own eyes.
The nightlife crawl from their homes
And steps from dens they are a-taking.
Inside the nightclubs loud and fierce,
All that noise they are making
And here we are in our own beds,
Involved in dreams from our own heads,
Until the morning when we rise,
To the sound of the songbird's cry.

Zoë Ward (11)
Wilmington Grammar School for Girls, Dartford

This Rose

A rose appears withered
Stands solely alone
In a field of bright colours
Standing dying alone

This is the rose
To which we are drawn
Not those brightly coloured
But the one that's alone

Beneath those dark colours
The rose is alive
More alive than the others
Though has apparently died

This rose is watered
Cared for and nourished
Unlike the others
This rose has flourished

As the pretty cries fade
Forgotten they die
This rose remains
Refusing to die

Its beauty renewed
Though it always was there
It matures and lives on
All it needed was care

Now there is a rose
Stands solely alone
Beautiful and proud
Stands triumphant alone.

Hannah Katsis (15)
Wilmington Grammar School for Girls, Dartford

A Man

I watched him leave
Every morning,
I watched him return
Every night.
That man, a man
With a family,
A man with a taste
For hops and barley,
A man who
Filled his lungs with
Suffocating, smouldering
Soot.
Inhaled for flimsy,
Standardised, scraps
Of paper,
That no one raises
To the light anymore,
Checking for its sincerity.
All this I have seen,
All this I know
Too well,
Yet the infinite
Cycle remains,
The perimeter
Unchallenged.
Only now it is me
Who inhales, not soot,
But the dust from
My office chair.
I do not cough.

Rebecca Ann Rieley (17)
Wilmington Grammar School for Girls, Dartford

The Middle Of The Night

Walking slowly,
In the middle of the night,
Unsure of what to believe.

This is what happened,
In the middle of the night.

Hearing my footsteps,
Echoing all around,
I hear a howl, a bark, a sound.

That's what I heard,
In the middle of the night.

I saw it coming,
Through the trees,
Shining in the light.

That's what I saw,
In the middle of the night.

I walked over,
Touched it
And felt its harsh breath on my skin.

That's what I felt,
In the middle of the night.

Then it disappeared
Like a flash,
Deep into the night.

That's what happened
In the middle of the night.

Emma Chandler (13)
Wilmington Grammar School for Girls, Dartford

A Leafy Tale

Long hot summer days are reaching an end,
The winds are gathering and the branches will bend.
Swaying through the sky so free,
Knowing the end is coming for me.
Nothing to stop the seasons from turning,
So here I am like bright orange burning.

Flicking through the branches wildly and madly,
The whistling gust of wind caught me so badly.
As I jolt and tremble to the ground,
I see raging reds of a fire mound.
I join the pile of reds, oranges and browns,
A strong gale could thrust us up and see us dance like clowns.

Here I am at last now brown and crunchy,
Waiting for little boots to trample and munch me.
I can feel the dew making me soft and smooth again,
Nothing to do but lay here intensely - oh what a pain
The autumn ends my life every year,
Just as spring returns all the time with a cheer.

Emily Williams (11)
Wilmington Grammar School for Girls, Dartford

Winter

The moon is a big bright glow
Lighting up the fresh white snow
In a glance and in a gleam
Over the land a bright white beam
The wild horses running free
Across the mountains hastily
For summer has left at last
Warm days a thing of the past.

Katherine Morris (13)
Wilmington Grammar School for Girls, Dartford

The Sun

The sun is an orange fire, heating the Earth's surface,
It breathes its light and lowers behind the hills,
Creating a beautiful sunset,
Blaring, like an explosion.

She awakens from her sleep and rises, back to work,
The calmness is shattered as she is locked up like a criminal,
The dense clouds are padlocks, securing her bars,
She boils out from her prison to light our world again.

She is the Earth's core in the desert,
Peering over the sand dunes at the rotting animal carcasses,
Water, burnt out, scarce,
The desert is a chicken, roasting in her clutches.

Kerry Brown (12)
Wilmington Grammar School for Girls, Dartford

School Bell Rings

School bell rings,
With pupils coming,
School bell rings,
With children chatting,
School bell rings,
With us pushing,
School bell rings,
With pupils rushing,
School bell rings,
With us moaning,
School bell rings,
With children running,
To get home at last.

Natalie Collcutt (11)
Wilmington Grammar School for Girls, Dartford

Violence!

Why is there violence?
For what?
Money, drugs, power,
Take your pick!

Violence is war and war is violence,
The mistakes made,
I can only think how bad the consequences are,
Homelessness, starvation, death.

People left for dead,
People who lost the ones they loved,
Filled with anger and hatred,
Wanting revenge, violent revenge,
Is that right?

Can't they see they would be no better than them?
Revenge, anger, pain,
This is what controls them,
This is what controls their enemy.

Fighting with guns, knives, tanks, is not the answer!
Try talking,
Did that not occur to you,
Or could you just not be bothered?
Did you just want your money, your power!

You can stop this,
Disputes, violence, what violence you could say,
All you will get is discomfort and death,
Stop this vicious circle, I say,
It will always lead you in the wrong direction,
The direction of disaster, you say.

Stephanie Nasskau (14)
Wilmington Grammar School for Girls, Dartford

The Blue Skies

The sunrise
The blue skies
And windy days

The heartbeat
Memories that we keep
Reminiscing about the old ways

One life to live
Many things to give
What we feel and cannot see

Places where we go
People that we know
It's all up to me

Choices that we make
All those mistakes
Beginning to adopt dreams

Different point of view
All is fake and true
In a world where nothing is as it seems

Appreciate the scenery
All is meaningful to me
The children in the distance play with delight

I see beauty in the dirt
I gain perseverance through the hurt
As the day turns to a magnificent night.

Alecia Cotterell (14)
Wilmington Grammar School for Girls, Dartford

My Baby Brother

My little brother is called Ben
January 11th - he was born then
He is only nine months old
At the moment he is still good as gold
His mum and dad are really proud
But he can be extremely loud
He's never really bad
Even when he is feeling sad
He loves to play with toys
Just like all the little boys
When his dad sings to him he giggles
When he is on the floor he always wriggles
He's got the cutest smile
I hope it's there for a while
He loves to play with his mummy
Especially when she tickles his tummy
Ben has a sister and brother
We all love each other.

Faye Baker (13)
Wilmington Grammar School for Girls, Dartford

The Fairy

She wore a gown of peace and light,
That stopped everyone who was in a fight.
It stopped the wars in the world
And all the abuse being hurled.
If you saw her dancing there,
You wouldn't have a single care.
But when she went away again,
Everything started, war and pain.

Charlotte Coates (11)
Wilmington Grammar School for Girls, Dartford

The War Of The Generations

When I was so young,
Maybe only five or six,
I used to watch the boys play war
With their machine guns going
Ch! Ch! Ch! Ch! Ch!
I used to think it was funny,
Seeing them fall to the ground
When they were shot.
But when I look back on it now,
It might be amusing,
But thinking about it,
Osama bin Laden, Saddam Hussein,
Adolf Hitler and many more, I am sure,
Wanted to take over or destroy this Earth.
Ch! Ch! Ch! Ch! Ch!
Argh!
That's what a real war sounds like.
A brutal battle,
Fighter jets against nuclear weapons
Life or death?
Civilisation or devastation?
All contained within the deciding bomb.
Will it be dropped?

Verity Adamthwaite (12)
Wilmington Grammar School for Girls, Dartford

The King Of Communication

The king of communication,
May be sold at pricey deals.
Including this money you must pay
It's called bills.
Even though this phone
Is smaller than your hand,
They could widen our social life,
Yes it could expand.
These mobile phones are helpful,
These mobile phones are strong,
These mobile phones can even
Play you a song.
They come in all different colours
And cases
This phone means we can talk to each other
From many other places!

Abigail Shepherd (11)
Wilmington Grammar School for Girls, Dartford

Night-Time

The moon was shining
In the midnight sky.
The clouds were watched
As time went by.
The stars were twinkling
Silver and bright
It was one hour past midnight.
The waves were leaping over the caves
The moon shone on the curling waves.
Swishing and swirling the sea curled
At night, a bright and beautiful world.

Katharine Sherlock (12)
Wilmington Grammar School for Girls, Dartford

If I Had A Pet

If I had a dog,
He would be so smart,
He would love me,
Deep down in his heart.

If I had a cat,
It would be so much fun,
We would go for walks,
Out in the sun.

If I had a hamster,
I would love it so,
He would follow me,
Wherever I go.

If I had a snake,
It would slither around,
It would go into my room,
But make no sound.

If I had a monkey,
He'd help me swing on a vine,
I'd bring him home,
He'd be all mine.

If I had a parrot,
We'd go to the park
And then listen,
To the song of the lark.

If I had a pet,
He'd really love me,
For my locked heart,
He'd be the key.

Manisha Sharma (11)
Wilmington Grammar School for Girls, Dartford

School

School isn't something you want to keep,
Classes make you fall asleep.
There's nothing that interests you,
You're constantly asking if you can go to the loo.
You fake you're ill in the middle of school,
When you're not exactly ill at all.
Teachers talk about nothing all day,
I don't see how they earn a week's pay.
We could build a house
With all the homework we get,
We use excuses like, 'Rex ate it, my pet.'
The end of school is always the best,
But dread tomorrow oh no!
It's a maths test!

Ellis Kitchener (11)
Wilmington Grammar School for Girls, Dartford

My Mum

My mum makes me happy
When the skies are grey,
My mum has a smile
That brightens up my day.

My mum's really groovy
She has very nice things,
She has cool clothes and cool shoes
And really gorgeous rings.

My mum is the best
And I love her to the moon,
I know that for her, in my heart,
I will *always* have room.

Paige Lidbury (11)
Wilmington Grammar School for Girls, Dartford

Heartbreak

Hearts are fragile and delicate,
They are easy things to break
And I know, because mine is now broken,
Or if not broken, then cracked.

Have you ever seen a bowl with a fine crack running through it?
Worthless? Useless?
That is what my heart is like now,
Just a solid ache to be carried in my chest.

And why did this happen I hear you ask,
Because I have been rejected, abandoned, forgotten,
By those whom I deemed friends,
Now the pain eats me alive.

The hurt would go away you know,
If I could convert my pain into anger,
But I can't,
I can't hate those I cared for.

I wish I could.
Hate is simple, easy,
It doesn't sting or burn,
But I don't.

So my heart stays broken.

Elizabeth Thacker (15)
Wilmington Grammar School for Girls, Dartford

Into The Eyes Of War

Crouching low, hiding from fighters overhead,
Sirens screaming deep into the deadly night.
Mothers and children cling tightly to each other, waiting for the end.
Fearful tears rolling down the cheeks of innocent children.
Streaking their dirt-covered faces.
Outside carnage and destruction,
Flames roaring ferociously, burning everything.
Bombs dropping like thunder.
Falling, falling into the darkness, presents from the Devil.
Will it ever stop?
Thoughts of death running through troubled minds,
As gunshots enter the soldiers' exhausted bodies.
Tanks rolling past, ignoring the dead,
Can't stop, can't feel, will weaken and bring danger.
Save only who will survive another battle.
Please help! They cry silently, wanting to go home.
Steel birds of Hell soar through the blackened sky,
Releasing their beasts of terror, ready to explode with chaos.
Slowly, it seems decades later they fade.
No more fuel so the fear has stopped.
But still it is barely safe.
Once again shy faces appear,
Only to have to cope with the devastation left behind.
But to be alive is a blessing.
God help us!

Hope Anscomb (13)
Wilmington Grammar School for Girls, Dartford

A Dream

The duvet lay twisted upon the floor
Hands clenching into clammy fists
The eerie silence broken by
The sound of rasping breathing.

The girl sat up, gave a piercing scream
Her eyes full of fearful tears
Sat there a moment, clutching the sheets
As if in a mystical trance.

Her knuckles were white from gripping the torch
As she crept silently across the landing
The shadows sent shivers down her spine
She held her breath as she peered through the door.

Wringing her hands and nodding her head
She told herself that she was safe
Carefully picked up her messy duvet
And slid cautiously back into bed.

She lay there like a block of ice
Breathing slow and steady
Did she sleep? She could not tell
The morning sun rose and melted her fear.

Laura Smith (13)
Wilmington Grammar School for Girls, Dartford

Self Portrait

There's a girl in the corner,
whose name I do not know.
With her nose in a book,
her face does not show.
She walks to school
with a look on her face,
as if she has lost
the fight for the human race.
Her wispy black hair
is as shiny as can be.
When it is out of a bun
it falls down past her knee.
Her father picks her up from school
and drives her home for supper.
You would think she has no money
as her shoes have lost their rubber.
So who is this girl?
Who could she be?
Yes! You've guessed it!
The girl is me.

Laura Cross (13)
Wilmington Grammar School for Girls, Dartford

My Walk

I went for a walk along the road,
I walked and walked and met a toad.
The toad jumped and vanished down my T-shirt
And all that I could hear was *ribbet, ribbet, ribbet.*

I carried on my walk on a racecourse,
I walked and walked and met a horse.
The horse ran off to find some hay
And all that I could hear was *neigh, neigh, neigh.*

I continued my walk in a bog,
I walked and walked and met a dog.
The dog ran off wagging his tail
And all that I could hear was *bail-wail, bail-wail, bail-wail.*

My walk took me next to a rubbish heap,
I walked and walked and met a sheep.
The sheep wandered off to be killed for meat
And all that I could hear was *bleat, bleat, bleat.*

I carried on my walk in a forest now,
I walked and walked and met a cow.
I looked at my watch, it was half-past two
And all that I could hear was *moo, moo, moo.*

I finished off my walk at my house,
I opened the door and there was a mouse.
The mouse looked like he was going to speak
But all that I could hear was *squeak, squeak, squeak.*

Anna Milne (11)
Wilmington Grammar School for Girls, Dartford

Animals

Dolphins splashing, jumping around,
While koala bears stay far from the ground.
Giraffes stand up high and tall,
As hippos bath in a mud pool.

Elephants like to stomp and splash,
While cheetahs whizz by like a flash.
Sharks snap and bite,
Sea creatures hide in fright.

Dogs slobber and bark,
While cats make their mark.
Snakes slide round on their bellies,
People sit inside and watch their tellies.

Monkeys hang around making noise,
While zebras give birth to girls and boys.
Bears have teeth hanging from their mouth,
While in the winter birds fly south.

Lions lie and watch their prey,
As sloths doze off and sleep all day.
Rabbits hop round and dig their holes,
Crabs walk sideways and nip people's toes.

Pigs roll around and fill themselves up,
While a dog gives birth to a furry pup.
Sheep walk round and wear fluffy coats,
Up a mountain lives a billy goat.

Kangaroos are hopping around,
While under water you can't hear a sound.
Starfish are stuck to the seabed,
As ducks on a pond wait to be fed.

People help animals everywhere,
People help animals as they care.

Samantha Mace (12)
Wilmington Grammar School for Girls, Dartford